GOD
with a
Sword
in His
Hand

Edward A Rutherford

ISBN: 1460949668
ISBN-13: 9781460949665

Contents

INTRODUCTION

We live in a world that is hard to understand. Just when we think, we have things down pat, when it seems we know what we are doing and why the things happen as they do, our lives are turned upside down by some inexplicable event. Then we have to start all over again trying to put our universe back into some rational order.

The problem with most of our thinking is that it is two-dimensional. We look at the natural world and ourselves and try to come up with some philosophy that will allow us to understand what in the world is going on.

There is another reality at work and unfortunately, most of us are blind to it. There is a spiritual dimension that impacts our natural world and us. Most people understand that there is a spiritual side of individuals but they fail to see that the spiritual dimension is having impact on the world around them.

This book deals with that very real spiritual realm and the forces at work not only in our lives but also in the natural world around us. The world we live in is constantly changing because it is under the influence of a cosmic struggle. A struggle that has a direct impact on our lives and the lives of those we love. We are a part of that struggle whether we know it or not. We can and should use all of our power and resource to insure that we are not victims of this war. Instead, that we become "victors" in our personal struggles and help our side win the war.

A cosmic struggle, warfare, and battles, these are strange words but they are realistic descriptions of what is taking place in our lives, in this world and in the spiritual realm. We are told that creation is in rebellion against God. It began when Satan tried to overthrow God. It continued when man was influenced by Satan to join in the rebellion. That rebellion continues today even though Jesus Christ has made a way for us to win over the power of Satan.

INTRODUCTION

Jesus Christ, at the cross, gave us the ability, the power, the authority and the resource to begin to overcome Satan and his forces. Jesus certainly gave us what we need to win the struggle in our own lives. He also gave the needed instructions to put together the forces that can redirect battle in this world and bring hope to billions of people who are now enslaved by the evil one. We can be a part of that great liberation movement. How? Well, that is what this book is all about.. our responsibility, our part in the battle, and how to win.

CHAPTER ONE

THE WARRIOR GOD

It is possible to be a good Christian, be in the will of God and doing all the right things, still face opposition, and have very real problems.

Joshua was a good man. He had succeeded Moses and was now leading Israel into the Promised Land. God had told Joshua that God Himself was giving them this land. The people had crossed over the river Jordan in a glorious procession marked by the miracle of God and had celebrated the fulfillment of God's great plan.

Suddenly, there ahead of them loomed the great walled fortress of Jericho. It was like nothing they had ever seen before. The walls of the city towered above them. Walled cities of this era many times would stand sixty feet in the air. The walls were so thick that homes were built into them. Atop the walls, armies could oversee the feeble efforts of an attack and could easily turn back almost any assault.

Israel had just come from one of the most powerful nations on earth. Egypt was a mighty nation but they had no walled cities like Jericho. Egypt depended on its highly mobile and strong armies to go forth and meet the enemy. Jericho was a shock to Joshua and his generals. Something had to be done. Jericho and its inhabitants stood squarely in the path of Israel and the fulfillment of the promise of God.

The people were looking to Joshua to tell them what to do. How will they remove this obstacle that blocks their path? Joshua had no idea how to conquer Jericho. It seemed an almost impossible task.

We are told that Joshua was seated in front of his tent. He must have been pondering, praying for help. Joshua looks up and there standing before him is a warrior. The warrior in battle dress with his sword in his hand stands looking down at Joshua. At first, Joshua must have thought the man was the enemy, a man from Jericho. Joshua comes to his feet. There is something about this warrior.

As Joshua draws closer to him he asks, "Are you for us or one of our adversaries?"

Then comes the strange reply, "Neither, But as the Captain of the Host of the Lord, I have now come."

Joshua falls on his face and begins to worship this warrior. Don't get the wrong idea. This is not an angel. Angels, the Lord's angels, do not accept worship. Only the Lord is worthy of worship. Joshua knows he is in the presence of the living God. Joshua calls him Lord.

The Captain of the Lord's Host tells Joshua to unloose his sandals because they stand on Holy Ground. Ground made Holy because this Captain of the Lord's Host stands there. Like Moses standing before the burning bush in the presence of the living God had to remove his shoes in holy reverence, Joshua has to remove his sandals. Joshua is in the presence of God. This warrior is neither a man nor an angel, He is God.

This is God who stands between Joshua and Jericho. This is God standing in His battle garments with His sword drawn. The Lord speaks to Joshua.

He says, "I give you this city, its king and its mighty warriors." Then the Lord gives Joshua a detailed plan to take Jericho. How they are to march around the city for seven days. On the seventh day, they are to blow the trumpets and give a great shout and Jericho will fall. Joshua is told to follow the plan to the smallest detail and the city will be theirs.

That is exactly what happened. Joshua and his armies did what the Lord had said. At the same moment it was promised the walls of the city fell. The walls fell not because of trumpets, not because of the shouts, but the hand of God felled the walls and Israel took the city.

This is an amazing picture of God. The Lord as a Warrior-God... God as a fellow soldier standing with His people in battle garb. There stands God with

His sword drawn and ready to lead His people into battle. There is our God with a sword in His hand.

LIFE IS A BATTLE

Here is a great truth we often miss. Life is a battle. Man is in the midst of a cosmic struggle. This is an analogy of our lives. This truth is seen over and over again in the Bible.

Paul made it clear in his letter to the church at Ephesus. In the sixth chapter, he said recognize your true enemy, we don't wrestle against flesh and blood but against spiritual powers. He goes on to give instructions as to how we are to put on our armor, pick up our weapons, and be ready for battle. The truth is simple. We are constantly in a war.

War is not pretty. Its effects are perplexing. Bombs dropping, shells bursting, bullets flying and it matters not who you are, if you are young or old, good or bad. One dies. Another is crippled. Sometimes, we forget about the war and then there is a tragedy. Someone we love is hurt or destroyed. We wonder why. They were so young. They were good. Why did this happen? War is ugly.

The enemy is doing battle with God over the very souls of men. He is a psychotic enemy that only wants to break the heart of God. We are told that God looks on us as His own children. He wants the best for us. If Satan can lead us astray, if he can cause us to do the wrong things, to fail God, he knows he can break God's heart. That is his goal. He wants to hurt God by hurting God's creation. He wants to corrupt God's handiwork.

Sin runs rampant in this world and sin destroys. Whether it is the drunk driver racing down the highway, or some dreaded disease loosed on the world through the fall of man, sin destroys. We live in a world where sin still abounds and where we can be hurt by the power of sin and its ultimate instigator Satan.

Is there really a devil? Do people really believe in a being that runs around in a red suit with a pitchfork like he has just escaped off a Tabasco bottle? No. Satan is not the comic caricature of our imagination. He is, in fact, a fallen angel. He is a created being who was once one of God's most precious beings. We are told that pride entered into his life and he thought he could replace God. What was once a wonderful, beautiful, glorious angel became a malignant horror intent on hurting the heart of God. Is Satan real? Yes, he is very real and he is intent on destroying you.

We are at war. What is at stake in this struggle is everything precious to you, including your loved ones, your community and this world. There is only one obstruction to Satan's total dominion of this world. The church, of Jesus Christ, armed with the power of God, ready to stand against the enemy.

The task is formidable, no, it is impossible in our own strengths. We are to do battle with Satan and win the freedom of our loved ones, our city and the world. Mark it out. God stands ready. He stands before us with His battle armor on, His sword drawn, ready to lead us into battle. Ready to fight with us so that we might take our city. Our Lord is mighty. He is the King of kings, the Lord of lords, who can stand before Him? Victory is assured. If we will only listen and follow His plan.

GOD'S PLAN

There are times we come up with our plans. We devise programs and strategies. Then we pray and ask God to help us accomplish our plans. Like Joshua, we stand before God, and ask are you for us or against us? That is never the question. The question is, are we for God or against Him? He is the Captain. We are to follow Him.

See, we should have no faith in man's plans. Man's plans can fail. They can presuppose the wrong aims, goals and strategies. Man's plans are destined to fail. God's plans, on the other hand, cannot fail. We must follow Him. We must seek His face. Find out His will and then do it. As we do, we go forth in His power and strength. No city can stand before Him. God is looking, seeking a people who will truly follow Him.

The church has been given a mandate to take back lost territory. It is a world given over to the enemy by rebellious man. Our concern is not just land; it is a lost and a dying people, who are in the hands of the enemy.

We have been given an anointing of God to accomplish this task. We have everything that is necessary to win the battle and to take the city for God.

Our Captain stands before us, He points to our city, and He says, "I give you this city and its inhabitants. Go forth and take it." Are we ready to follow Him?

WHAT MUST WE DO?

There is a story. It is about an incident at a great university in the United States. At one time, this school which was, founded by a great Christian denomination, stood proudly for Christ. Times had changed. The university had a yearly lecture schedule and would invite the great speakers of the day to come and share with the faculty and students. One year, they invited a man who had come to great fame. The only problem was that he was an atheist. He agreed to come but demanded that he be allowed to speak to the point that there was no God. The administration, though reluctant but wanting this famous man to grace their campus, agreed.

The speaker was one of those gifted individuals. The moment he came to center stage he had won the affection of the audience. His words, wit, and charisma soon had the audience eating out of his hand. At the close of his speech, he made a challenge. Would anyone dare stand and challenge the assertions he just made? Would anyone stand and debate him on the existence of God? Some there disagreed, but this man was so gifted, such an orator they were afraid to stand. They knew that with his intellect he would cut their arguments to pieces.

The man scanned the crowd. He looked over the faculty, the students, but no one stood. He started to laugh, when suddenly, up in the balcony of the great hall, stood a little wisp of a girl. The crowd was a buzz, and the speaker could see the girl's lips moving, but couldn't hear what she was saying over the crowd noise.

He called out, "Quiet, I can't hear her."

There was a hush over the audience. You could hear her words, floating across the hall. She was singing.

"Stand up, stand up for Jesus, you soldiers of the cross.."

An old professor heard the words. They took him back to the times in church when he would be sitting next to his mother as she sang that grand old song. He began to feel the tears on his cheek and he stood to his feet joining in with the young girl.

"Stand up, stand up for Jesus.."

A young college student, who had been raised in church, but had allowed his new friends to lead him away from the Lord, felt the convicting power of God, and jumped to his feet singing. All over the crowd, people got to their feet and joined in, until soon nearly everyone was one their feet, in a resounding voice as one, singing,

"Stand up, stand up for Jesus.."

The speaker looked at the young girl, slammed his notebook shut and briskly walked off the stage. As he walked off the campus to his car, he could hear that song wafting across the campus.

"Stand up, stand up for Jesus, you soldiers of the cross.."

We need to take a stand. Christians must stand up in the face of the onslaught of the enemy. We are allowing Satan to take our freedom, our rights, and our loved ones. We must stand up and take our place in the battle lines. We are at war and every Christian is needed to take their God ordained position in the church.

It does not take great gifts, wonderful talents to serve Christ. This battle is for the willing. For those who will listen to God, stand up and take their place in the ranks of God's army. Yes, we have an enemy and he is doing his best to destroy people, but we can win. We must know what God expects of us. We need to learn how to recognize the enemy, his strategies and we must learn how to defeat him. We can win.

CHAPTER TWO

GETTING THE BIG PICTURE

A friend of mine from Indonesia told of his home village and the problems his people experienced because of an evil tree. This tree had an oddity in the trunk that looked like the face of some monstrous old man. The people of the village would offer sacrifice to the tree and the crops would flourish, things would go well. If they failed to sacrifice at the tree bad things would happen. My friend, now a very strong Christian, said as a young person that he could feel the power of the tree spirit.

A strange story, but not so strange, when we begin to come to understand the big picture. We live in a world that is under the power of sin. Sin permeates every sphere of life in this present age. If you have doubts merely read the daily newspaper, watch the television news or drive down the streets of any major city. See, we must ask the question, whose world is this?

WHOSE WORLD IS THIS?

If we believe the bible, then we should know that this world belongs to Satan. Let's go back to the temptation of Jesus. Jesus had been baptized and the Holy Spirit has descended upon Him. He begins an unusual spiritual journey by going on an extended fast and then is led into the wilderness where Satan tempts him. One of the temptations that Satan uses is that he offers Jesus all the kingdoms of the world. He showed Him the world and its glory and then said, "All these things I will give you if you will fall down and worship me."

For this temptation to be real, Satan had to have the world to offer. Jesus doesn't challenge Satan's authority over the world, instead He quotes Deuteronomy 6:13, that we should only worship God. The truth is that this world is under the power of Satan and has been since the fall of man, that we, humankind, turned the world over to the devil the moment we sinned.

Listen to Jesus, in John 12:31, as He speaks of Satan and his ultimate end when the Day of Judgment comes. Jesus calls Satan, "the ruler of this world..." The world belongs to the devil. He rules this world and its inhabitants. He is hard at work destroying lives and keeping people in bondage.

We can see this further as Satan is described in the New Testament. Paul, in his second letter to the Corinthians (4:4), calls Satan, "the god of this age..." Paul is saying that Satan rules the hearts of the unsaved, that he controls their lives, even though they are unaware of it, that the lives of the unsaved are a form of worship to the devil. We all serve some god.

Paul further elaborates in Ephesians 2:2. He refers to Satan as the prince of the power of the air. That designation again points to his domination over this world and its inhabitants. This also points to the idea that the spiritual realm exists all around us, that there are forces at work every moment, in every place, in our lives.

The bottom line is that this world, its kingdom and its people belong to Satan. The Bible makes it abundantly clear in the first letter of John 5:19,

"The whole world is under the control of the evil one." On a day-to-day basis, Satan is causing men and women to act in ways they wouldn't if they were not under his control. As a non-Christian, did you ever do something and then wonder why you acted like that? The King James Bible says, "The whole world lies in wickedness..." What a tragic picture. What are we going to do about it?

THE POWER OF CHRIST AND THE CHURCH

We have a God in heaven who cares about His creation and who has made it very clear that He loves humankind. Our Father in heaven sent His Son to break the bondage and the power of sin. We are told again in I John 3:8, that Jesus came to destroy the works of the devil. Jesus came to set men free, to establish His kingdom and to bring forth a group of people, the church, who would serve Him by continuing His work.

Christ did all of that at the cross and before He ascended into heaven, He gave the church its marching orders to continue the work of liberation.

Understand this, Jesus in His life and in His ministry showed His total domination over the powers of darkness. Whenever Jesus was confronted by demonic people He set them free.

What was the source of His power over evil spirits? It was not His deity. Philippians 2:5-8, makes it clear that Jesus laid aside His glory when he became flesh. Paul says that Jesus emptied Himself of His glory. He did not change His nature. He was still God, but He did not use the glory or the power of His deity to refuse sin or to overcome evil.

No, it wasn't because He was the Son of God. We have to go back to Luke 4:1, 14, back to the temptation to understand His authority over Satan and his forces.

Before Jesus was tempted, He had been filled with the Holy Spirit. He went forth and faced the trial of His faith. He overcame not by His own deity or authority but through the power of the Holy Spirit. In Luke 4:14, the Bible describes His return as it had when He had ventured forth into the wilderness. It says He returned, "Full of the Holy Spirit..."

Jesus made it clear where He got His power. In Matthew 12:24, the Pharisees challenge Jesus. The Pharisees claim that Jesus casts out evil spirits through the power of Satan. Jesus answers by identifying the source of His power. Jesus asks the rhetorical question, "If I cast out demons by the Spirit of God, surely the kingdom of God has come upon you." Jesus was saying that He cast out demons not by His own power but by the power of the Holy Spirit. In John 5:19, He said, "I do nothing of myself but I do what I see the Father in heaven do." Jesus had power over Satan because He was anointed by the Holy Spirit.

Peter in preaching to Cornelius' household said the same thing (Acts 10:38), "God anointed Jesus of Nazareth with the Holy Spirit and with power, who went about doing good and healing all who were oppressed by the devil, for God was with Him." Peter is saying Jesus didn't do these things by His own power or by His deity but through the power of the Holy Spirit."

JESUS EMPOWERS THE CHURCH

Jesus not only confronted and defeated the powers of darkness; He made a way for His church to continue to do the same thing. Paul describes Jesus' work on the cross in Colossians 2:15, "Having <u>disarmed</u> principalities and powers, He made a public spectacle of them, <u>triumphing</u> over them in it (the cross). At the cross, Jesus defeated Satan. Paul says Jesus disarmed the enemy. He took away the enemy's power over us who believe and who recognize what has taken place. In every war, there is a battle that decides the ultimate outcome. That battle is the turning point of the war. The cross was the decisive battle, the power of Satan's kingdom was destroyed, but the war goes on. The war has been decided. We are past the turning point but we must continue to fight until the final victory has been won.

Before Jesus ascended to His rightful place in heaven, He made a promise to the disciples and to all those who would end up following them. He said He would send the "promise" of the Father, the Holy Spirit. That the Holy Spirit would come and help us to continue the work that Jesus began. He went so far as to say that even greater works we would do. We need the Spirit's help to fight and to win against our enemy.

Jesus was pointing to the church and saying I have a task for you to do. You are to continue to destroy the works of the devil. You are to make known the gospel message, to show others the way to salvation, to teach them how to live glorious, victorious lives. He told those who saw him ascend those who had been with him in the upper room, to wait on the promise and that they would receive "power." They did and the church was empowered on the day of Pentecost to go forth and do battle.

We, who believe, have been empowered to fight and defeat the enemy. Believers are called to continue to establish the church and to continue to build the kingdom of God. That it is our task to set people free from the bondage of sin. We must never forget that we are fighting over the souls of men and women. We are doing battle with the minions of Satan. This is serious business and we must be about the work that Jesus has called us to do.

THE CHURCH HAS TO FIGHT THE SPIRITUAL BATTLE

We need to recognize that the church has been given a direct command by Jesus to share the message of faith and to lead others to a saving knowledge of Christ's grace. We need to understand that we, the church, are the only hope the world has for deliverance. It is not easy. It is hard to share our faith. It is hard to communicate the truth to a people enslaved by the kingdom of darkness. Satan is doing his best to keep people blind and deaf to the truth.

Some people question the validity of Mark 16, but the reality of the message cannot be questioned. We need to be about the business of the church. We must be snatching people from the bondage of Satan. We must see people's lives changed by sharing the truth of the gospel. We need to learn to witness. We need to be willing to invite others to attend church with us. We must open our hearts and our homes to those who do not know Jesus so that they can see that Christians are real people who know who they are and where they are going.

The church needs to be in the business of casting out devils and healing the sick. God hasn't changed; the Bible makes that clear in Hebrews 13:8, but the church has. We have been empowered to cast out demons, to set people free from the bondage of sin and to change lives.

Demons in America? Yes, they are all around us. They are hard at work in the lives of the unsaved, still about the business of the devil to maintain his dominion over their lives. If we don't break his power, if we don't pull down his strongholds, if we don't fight for the souls of men, we are not going to see lives changed.

Churches stand on street corners half empty because the people of God are not fighting the fight of faith. People are sitting in their homes, out golfing or doing a thousand other things and they and those they love are in bondage and heading toward total destruction and don't even know it. They need to see and experience a church that is alive with the power of God. A church where lives are touched by the presence of the Spirit of God, where people are being healed and set free from the oppression of the enemy. A church like that will not stand half-empty for long.

We must be willing to fight the spiritual battle. The church today needs people who will recognize that they are in a war. That we live in a world dominated by Satan and that if we don't stand up and do something then souls are going to be lost. The truth is our inaction; our unwillingness to fight the fight of faith will consign men and woman to hell for the lack of knowledge.

This is a war. Not a war fought with carnal weapons but one fought in the spiritual realm. This is a war that begins with Christians getting on their knees, before God and praying, "Lord, please open my eyes. Lord, help me to see and recognize the enemy at work. Then help me to pray. To pray like you did, Jesus, in the garden, praying 'great drops of blood' kinds of prayer. Those kinds of prayers will pull down the very fortresses of hell."

A TOUGH QUESTION FOR CHRISTIANS

What are you doing to upset the devil? Are Satan and his imps, his minions watching you and laughing. What are you doing to upset the devil's plans for your family, your neighbors, your co-workers and your community?

Are you simply living the Christian life? Are you just going to work, coming home, watching a little television and going to church? If you are not actively praying against the powers of darkness, if you are not on the front lines sharing your faith, if you are not actively working for the cause of Christ, then Satan doesn't care if you are a Christian. You are no threat to Him or to his work.

Let's get busy and do what Jesus has called us to do!

CHAPTER THREE

WHO RULES OUR NATION

At times, we Christians struggle with the direction our nation is taking. We get concerned about which political party rules the government, the policies, and the plans of our leaders. The Bible is clear; we are to pray for those who are in authority over our country, that our individual peace and our national well-being are determined by our willingness to pray for those in authority.

On the surface, it would appear that such prayers are significant but not life determining. We have to look beyond the apparent. The direction of our nation, the spiritual climate and our national future are not simply in the hands of politicians. Our world is under the sway of the evil one and our national direction can, unbeknownst to its political leaders, be influenced by satanic forces. The question we must consider is do evil spirits rule nations and cities and if they do what must we do about it.

THE FALSE GODS OF THIS WORLD

There is an amazing portion of scripture found in Deuteronomy 32:8. It speaks of the time when God divided the nations. God moved to separate the people into various groups, nationalities and peoples. This verse says that God divided the boundaries according to the number of the children of Israel. That seems odd. Why would God divide the world based on the number of people in Israel? Neither then nor later is there any indication that Israel would rule the whole world. This is not a reference to the division of Canaan. What is this all about?

The Septuagint translates this scripture as "according to the angels of God." This could indicate that angels were assigned to nations. Their purpose or goals are not clearly defined but it is easy to surmise that the angels were given authority over the nations.

They oversaw, protected or in some way cared for the development, moral and otherwise, of their specific areas of responsibilities.

We know Satan and one third of the angels rebelled against God. God in His power could have destroyed the rebellious but instead He allowed evil to exist to fulfill His greater plan. God allows evil to exist to bring forth a people who will of his or her own free will choose to follow God. The fallen spirits still fight against God and His creation. They are trying to hurt God by hurting His creation. Some of these evil spirits, with the indifference or the help of man, have overthrown some of the angels who oversaw various nations. How do we know that?

Daniel (10:10-21) tells of an angelic appearance. Daniel had been seeking the Lord in prayer. Suddenly an angel appears with God's answer. The angel tells Daniel that he had been delayed in bringing the answer to Daniel because he had been attacked, held back by another spiritual power who ruled over the nation of Persia. Obviously, this spiritual power was evil because it opposed the will of God. If God divided the nations according to angels and now an evil angelic being ruled over a nation, Persia, then the angel of God must have been deposed, removed or defeated. Therefore, there are evil spirits that attempt to rule over nations, cities and territories.

In the writings of the Old Testament, we see many references to false gods. Some are named. Others are identified by their geographical location. They are called the gods of Canaan or Egypt or simply the gods of the hills, the high places or the groves. This would indicate that these false gods reigned in certain areas and over the inhabitants of that land. The idols, the carved figures and trees cut into the images of gods were symbolic of the spiritual powers that worked behind them. That is why God insisted that the idols in high places be destroyed and rejected.

You get the full flavor for this in 2 Kings 17:9-17, where the history of Israel worshiping other gods is recounted. In verse 16, the writer speaks of molded and wooden images used to symbolize the "host of heaven" or fallen angels and the false god Baal. The children of Israel, when they took these so-called gods as their own, were actually worshiping evil spirits. The horror of idolatry, is not simply rejection of God, it is the giving of oneself over to a satanic spirit intent on hurting or destroying the very one who worships it.

There are other references to evil spirits ruling over lands, nations and cities. In I Kings 20:23, we see the Syrians declaring that their god is a god of the plains and that the God of Israel is a God of the hills. They identified territorial boundaries and spheres of influence to their gods. The Syrians soon discovered in their resounding defeat that the Lord God reigns in all creation. It isn't just the Old Testament that speaks of evil spirits influencing nations or lands and it is not just nations that come under the power of Satan.

COULD A SATANIC SPIRIT BE RULING OVER YOUR COMMUNITY?

In the New Testament there is a unique verse found in Revelation 2:13. It speaks of the ancient city of Pergamos. John, anointed by the Holy Spirit, says Pergamos is the city where Satan dwells, that in fact,

Satan's throne or place of government was in that city. Pergamos had become the center of satanic influence in the world. Evil spirits are intent on carrying out the will of Satan. They are at work to destroy people. They know that God aches over His wayward creation. Demons relish the opportunity to hurt God.

One way to fulfill their plan is to have rule over the governments that influence people's lives. Another way is to control and influence the geographical territory. Evil spirits do their best to create an oppressive atmosphere, to control the spiritual environment in such a way as to diminish the impact of the gospel. It is the application of the term the "kingdom of darkness," where evilness becomes so strong that it can be felt and impact the natural world.

We must recognize that this battle is not just for souls. We are fighting to take back the cities that Satan has stolen from the hands of God's people. If you doubt that cities or certain parts of cities are in the hands of Satan drive into the inner city of almost any large metropolitan center. You will see drugs being sold, prostitution and a myriad of other social problems. More than that, you can feel the oppressive forces of evil at work.

Paul, in Ephesians 6:12, describes the spiritual battle. He says we are in a struggle. We wrestle not against flesh and blood, people, but we have spiritual enemies. He describes our foes. He calls them principalities, powers, rulers of the darkness of this age, a host of wickedness in the heavenly places. He is saying that our warfare is against individual spirits and against those who rule nations, cities and other territories.

We must understand that these spirits not only fight against us individually, they influence governments, and they direct nations to hinder the plans of God. History is full of incidents where the cruelty of man surpasses our understanding. There are cities and nations that seem to have become the very cesspools of evilness, governments that seemed to have been directed by Satan himself. If we are to succeed in changing the world, we must recognize that we have to take our nations and our communities back.

We have an example of how to do that in Paul's experience in establishing the church in the city of Ephesus. Ephesus was a city dominated by the cultic worship of the goddess Diana. In Acts, chapter 19, we are given insight into the battle against this evil spirit that ruled Ephesus and its neighboring territory.

EPHESUS AND THE GODDESS DIANA

Ephesus was the third largest city in the Roman Empire. It was a city that was the center of the worship of the black arts. People would travel to Ephesus to obtain special oils, amulets and idols. They would go to those versed in the black magic and purchase "spells" to affect others or to change their own lives. Most of this trade in the occult centered around the great Temple of Diana. The Temple was one of the wonders of the ancient world. It was made of black marble and onyx and towered over the city.

In Acts 19:27, the Ephesians boasted that all of Asia and the world worshiped Diana. People would come from all over Asia to worship at the Temple and buy spiritual favors. In verse 35, we are told that Diana's image had come down from heaven. It has been recorded in other ancient writings that miracles and wonders took place in the temple. The apocryphal book, The Acts of Andrew, says that there was a rock in the temple of Diana that was the home of demonic spirits. These demons would manifest themselves in ways that made people believe in the powers of the goddess Diana.

Paul came into the city preaching the good news. We are told he stayed in the area for two years and that all heard the gospel. Paul's ministry was anointed by the Holy Spirit. In verses 11-20, we are given a description of the impact of the gospel on Ephesus. Paul not only preached, his ministry was accompanied by miracles. Even the things that Paul wore or touched were used to heal and cast out evil spirits. Paul's ministry was changing the city. Not only were many saved and healed, but also they brought the tools of their practice of black magic and burned them.

The people of Ephesus became afraid. This message of life was setting people free. They were no longer under the influence of the evil spirits that reigned behind the worship of Diana. Even after stirring up a riot, the followers of Diana couldn't stop the work of Christ. When Paul left Ephesus, he left a strong church that had influence throughout Asia Minor.

Satan has a plan. In Second Corinthians 4:4, Paul tells of what Satan is trying to do. Satan is trying to keep the minds of the unsaved "blind" to the "light" of the gospel. That is why we must fight to share the gospel with people. However, he also has a larger agenda. In Revelation 20:3, we are told that Satan is going to be put away in the bottomless pit for a period of time, so that he can no longer "deceive the nations."

Satan is presently deceiving nations. He is controlling governments and nations both through his puppets and by creating an atmosphere of evil darkness that oppresses the work of the church. Nazi Germany is a historical example. There were good people in Germany during the rise of Nazism. There were Christians who opposed the horrible crimes committed against the Jewish people. Many who stood up ended up in prison or they were branded as traitors and executed. The good people, the Christians, those who opposed Hitler could do nothing. The nation, the majority of the people were deceived and the work of God was thwarted.

IF YOU ARE GOING TO CHANGE THE WORLD...

Daniel was a man who saw his prayers answered. It was not without a battle. The prince of Persia opposed the work of God. It took time but Daniel saw the answer to his prayers. How did he do it?

FIRST, HE PREPARED HIMSELF FOR BATTLE.

In Daniel (9:3), we see Daniel made up his mind that he was going to hear from God. He prepared himself. He said, "I set my face toward the Lord God..." Daniel was determined to hear from God. He wanted answers. He wanted God to restore his people and he wanted to understand how it was going to be done. We need to know God's plan. We need to understand how to accomplish it.

THEN, HE PRAYED AND FASTED.

Prayer is becoming a lost treasure in the church. Prayer that makes a determination that it is going to lay hold of the living God. He fasted. Fasting not as a lever to get God to hear or to answer but to prepare him to hear and understand. It was a fast to deny the flesh, the carnal nature of man and to strengthen the spiritual side of our lives.

HE CONFESSED HIS SINS AND THE SINS OF HIS PEOPLE.

Daniel recognized that he was a sinner. That he needed God's help not just for the task he was doing, but also even to have a relationship with God. He also asked God to forgive his nation for their corporate sins. We need to seek God's blessing on our nation. We should all pray and ask God to bless our country. However, first, we should ask God to forgive our nation. Forgive us for not serving Him, for acting presumptuously, for the many, many sins we corporately commit against him daily.

HE PERSEVERED.

In Daniel 10:2, we are told that Daniel kept on praying. Not for an hour, a day, a week, he prayed for three weeks. He kept on praying until he got an answer. How would the world change if we kept praying until we got an answer? Paul, in speaking of the spiritual battle in Ephesians (6:13-14), makes it clear. He says, "Stand... And keep on standing..." We are in a war. If we are going to change our city, our nation, our world, we had better be ready to fight and to keep on fighting.

WHAT MUST WE DO

You are in a war. You have been called into God's army. You have a very real enemy. He is fighting against you and wants to destroy you, everyone, and everything that you love. He controls this present world. He is influencing your national leaders, the policies of your government and the spiritual environment of your country. He reigns over cities, towns, neighborhoods and probably influences every place you might go.

Most people, most Christians are oblivious to Satan and to his destructive work. We must wake up. We have a fight on our hands. As Christians, the battle is not optional. You are in the fight. The only choices are to get run over, beat up and see all that we love destroyed or to fight back and win.

Prepare yourself to seek God. Pray and fast. Ask God to open your eyes and understanding that you might see Satan's hand at work, so that you can oppose it. Begin to ask God to help you pull down the strongholds in your community. Pray for our government leaders. Ask God to protect them from evil influences. Ask the Lord to guide them even if they don't know Him. Let them believe it is their own idea but let God's will and plan be done in our community, our city and our nation.

CHAPTER FOUR

TAKING OUR NATION BACK

While serving as Pastor in the Los Angeles area, we received a letter from a pastor in the northern part of Los Angeles County. It was a letter of warning. In the letter, the pastor related how a young man, who had previously lived in our community, had moved to his area and had become a Christian.

The young man had been involved with a satanic cult in our city. This cult would gather and call on the forces of evil to destroy our church. This was not just on cultic high days but they were continually binding themselves together to empower and release the resource of hell against the church.

We knew that cultic activity was taking place in our city. It was reported in the newspapers that police and sheriff departments found animal sacrifices, pentagrams, and other satanic symbols and objects. A local cemetery had been desecrated and a makeshift altar had been found at the scene.

We knew that the church was under attack and that the work of Christ was being hindered. What we didn't know was that the Satanists were spending as much time in attempting to curse the church as we were in prayer. We had a battle on our hands and until we became as concerned about the struggle as our enemy did, we wouldn't make much progress.

There are forces at work that want to hinder the advance of the kingdom of God. They want to stop the church's ministry. They want the church to fail. They are hard at work.

The question becomes what are we going to do about it.

HOW TO CONQUER A CITY

Jesus speaks directly to the warfare we face. In the book of Revelation Chapters 2 and 3, Jesus speaks to the seven churches of Asia Minor. There are seven different messages. Each message has some things in common. All describe the author of the messages as Jesus and each affirms a dynamic truth. Each message states the Spirit says, He commands, that the church is to **overcome.** Obviously, this is a crucial matter for the church. What are they to overcome? From the context and historically, we know the churches of Asia were under siege from Satan. Christians were persecuted, jailed and even murdered for their beliefs. Evil, the forces of Satan were at work against the church.

This word "overcome" is a military term. In the Greek, it means to conquer. Why use this word in this context? John the revelator was emphasizing that the church, believers, are in a spiritual battle. This word and its context presuppose the conflict that exists between God and the demonic powers of Satan. The word, "nikao", is found in two other places.

In Luke 11:22, Jesus is speaking directly to defeating demonic forces. Jesus has been challenged by the religious community. Jesus has cast out a demon. There are those who say that Jesus has done this by the power of Satan. Jesus uses the analogy of someone trying to take something from a strong person. Jesus says that one cannot defeat a strongman and take away his goods unless he first "overcomes" that strongman. He uses this same word. In spiritual warfare, we must overcome a strong enemy if we want to win the battle.

In John (16:33), again speaking directly to the battle at hand, Jesus warns the disciples. Jesus has told His disciple that the time is at hand. He is facing the cross. He knows that the disciples will be scattered in fear. They will face tribulation. Jesus encourages them. He tells them, "overcome." Yes, you will face trials, persecution, attacks from Satan but overcome and win the battle, you can do it.

Jesus is telling us the same thing in the book of Revelation. We are at war. We have an enemy who wants to defeat us. We must fight. Not just fight, we must fight and WIN. As you read the messages to the churches, you will see promises of great reward made. If the churches obey, if they **overcome**, they will receive great blessing. They will eat of the tree of life (2:7), they will not be hurt by the second death (2:11), they will eat of hidden manna (2:17), they have power over nations (2:26) and on and on. These are wondrous rewards to those who hear and overcome.

To take a city we must fight And win. We are in the fight. We have no choice. Once we became believers, we became part of the army. The only choice we have is to win or lose. The stakes are high. We are fighting for the souls of men, women and children. We must fight to win. We must enter into the spiritual battle for the souls.

SATAN IS AT WORK IN OUR CITY

Satan has a long-term agenda. He wants to stop people from being saved. Remember, Satan's goal is to break the heart of God, by dragging men into sin, degradation and failure. Satan wants to keep them lost. In Second Corinthians 4:4, Paul speaks directly to the mission of the god of this world. The god of this world is, of course, Satan. Satan's mission is to keep lost humanity "blind" to the light of the gospel. Why? So that, they won't come to the saving knowledge of Jesus Christ. Satan does not want people who are not Christians to hear that God really loves them and has made a way for them to be saved.

It is Satan's goal to keep people and human society as miserable as possible. Jesus said in John 10:10, that our enemy has come to steal, kill and destroy. Jesus went on to say that He has come to bring life, not just life, but an abundant life, one rich in the blessings of God.

A SIMPLE MESSAGE OF SALVATION

The church has the greatest message the world has ever heard. It has to be told. It is so simple. It is as easy as ABC.

1. **A - <u>Acknowledge</u>** your need for a savior. I have sinned and need my life changed.

2. **B - <u>Believe</u>** on the Lord Jesus Christ. I believe that God the Father sent His Son to die for my sins and raised Him up again to reign forever.

3. **C - <u>Confess</u>** Jesus as your Lord and Savior. I ask Jesus to come into my life. I put my sins on the cross and I receive the righteousness of God. I give Jesus His rightful place in my life as my Lord.

In a simple and direct prayer, we not only receive salvation but the promise of the best possible life we can have in this world.

The church must be about the work of Christ. Lest we forget, we have been given a commission, in Matthew 28:19, by the Lord Jesus Christ. We have been called to snatch men and women from the hold of Satan. To share this message of true liberation that sets people free. A message that opens blinded eyes to the truth. God is not some petty tyrant waiting for them to fail. God is a loving father wanting to reach out to His rebellious children, restore them to their proper position, and give them the best possible existence in this world and the promise of eternal life.

Why isn't the church doing what God has called us to do? Satan is hard at work. He is fighting the work of the church. He is fighting against individual Christians. We find ourselves in places of struggle. We, too often, simply accept it and say something like, its providence, bad luck, and fate. No, it is Satan doing his best to make you miserable.

SATAN'S PLAN TO KEEP CHRISTIANS UNDER CONTROL

Satan wants Christians to be self-centered. If the devil and his forces can get Christians more concerned about themselves than about others, he has won a great victory. The devil's plan is to get us to center our thoughts and prayers on our own condition. It becomes, "Lord help me, I want, I need, or oh, bless me." Do you want to know how to get what you want? Get concerned about others. That is what Christianity is, it is serving and helping others. It is looking outward not inward. It is Loving God with all your mind, heart and soul and others as yourself. It is an outward-reaching love that comes through a heart that has been filled with the love of God. We need to pray for others, care about others, minister to others. As we do that God will bless us.

Understand this, Satan is very organized. In Ephesians 6:11-12, we are told that our battle is against principalities, powers, rulers of wickedness in high places. Paul is speaking of a spiritual hierarchy. That when Satan fell, he took with him a group of rebellious angels. They established a force that is well organized. It is an organization that acts and carries out the goals of Satan.

We speak of Satan attacking us but we recognize that it is his forces at work. That is his plan against you, your family, your church may be carried out by some imp or demon, some subordinate of the evil one. It is still his plan, his ultimate goals, so we refer to him, Satan, as the one behind it, as the one working against us. It may be that a specific demon has been assigned to bring all hell against you. His task is to keep you miserable, to steal, to destroy, to kill, if possible. The fight is on. What are you going to do?

WARFARE IN THE HEAVENLIES

How should we fight? What do we do to overcome this enemy? We have a case history. It is found in Daniel chapter 10.

Daniel is a spiritual leader of Israel. He is a prophet in a foreign land. The nation of Israel has fallen into the hands of the Babylonians. Israel for years had rejected the love of God. God had allowed hardship, destruction and ultimately domination by another country to cause Israel to see the folly of serving false gods and self. In Daniel Chapter 10, we see Daniel seeking the face of God. He wants answers about the future. He has committed himself to a time of prayer and intercession to hear from God.

While He is praying an angel appears to him. The angel tells Daniel about a remarkable incident. He says that he has come from the very throne of God with an answer to Daniel's prayer. While the angel was on his way with the answer, he found himself confronted by a satanic angel. This evil angel withstood or fought against the angel of God. This evil angel is then identified as the "Prince of Persia of the Air".

It is important to see what caused this battle in the heavens. It was Daniel's prayers that caused God to send forth the angel. If Daniel hadn't prayed the answer would not have been sent. This cosmic struggle was brought about by Daniel's prayers. It is also important to see the time frame. Daniel did not just pray one time and wait on the answer. He kept on praying. He kept seeking God. If he had only prayed once would he have received the answer?

Notice that this evil spirit that fought against Daniel was identified with the nation of Persia. This spirit had the responsibility from Satan to rule over this nation and its territories. This spirit was powerful because the nation was exerting its influence through conquest. This spirit probably oversaw many other subordinate spirits with its sphere of influence. Yet it was this spirit that directly opposed the will of God for Daniel's life.

Remember Daniel was attempting to understand and make known the will of God for his people. He was building the kingdom of God. Daniel was a threat to the work of Satan against Israel and especially in the rebuilding of Jerusalem. This spirit was attempting to withhold the answers until Daniel would give up. Daniel could not get the answer until this spirit was defeated. The great news is that Daniel kept on praying and seeking the face of God until he got an answer. That should speak to us.

We must be people of prayer. We cannot simply say a few words to God and then expect to go out walking in victory. Prayer is our means of laying hold of God and His power. We must make prayer our first and foremost priority.

This is important; we must recognize that God has called us to do a work in this world.

GOD HAS GIVEN US AUTHORITY TO FIGHT

In the beginning of the book of Jeremiah we are told of the prophet's call to the work of God. Jeremiah was afraid when God called him to ministry. He thought he didn't have what it took to do the job. Most of us can identify with that. God spoke to Jeremiah to encourage him. God told the young prophet not to be afraid that the Lord would give him the words to speak and that He would be with him to deliver him.

Then God gave a Jeremiah a charge. God put forth His hand and touched Jeremiah's mouth. The Lord then spoke, "Behold, I put my words in your mouth. See, I have this day set you over nations and over kingdoms, to root out and to pull down, to destroy and to throw down, to build and to plant."

These are strange words to speak to Jeremiah. Jeremiah was not a king or a leader of the armies. He does not lead or encourage Israel to conquer other nations or kingdoms. You see this "charge" had nothing to do with the physical world. Jeremiah was a prophet. He was given spiritual authority. He was being sent forth to do the work of God. Notice the order of things in these orders given to the prophet. He was to build and to plant but first he had other work to do. What kind of work? Preparatory work of fighting the enemy who ruled over the places he was to build.

God gave Jeremiah spiritual authority over nations and kingdoms. Nations and kingdoms then ruled by the powers of darkness. Jeremiah was told to go and root out the enemy. Find the enemy then pull down their strongholds, destroy and throw down. Then he could begin to build and to plant.

God has called His people to do a work to go out and build great churches. To build Churches that can proclaim the truth to their communities, Churches that can manifest the glory of God to a lost generation looking for answers. Churches that can change not just their community, their city but that can change the world. To do that, first, we must go to war in the heavens. We must defeat our enemy. We must pull down his stronghold and put his minions to flight. The great truth is we can do it.

CHAPTER FIVE

EQUIPPED TO WIN THE BATTLE

In the book of James 4:7-8, we are given four instructions about spiritual warfare. James is speaking to believers. James is writing to Christians and telling them how to win in their battles against the devil. He is giving them instructions about how to take their places in the battle lines. James is telling us how to be warriors for Christ and put the enemy to flight. We need this. That is why we grab a hold of "Resist the devil and he will flee from you."

The other three instructions are the key to being able to resist and having the authority to see Satan flee. These three commands speak directly to our relationship with the Lord. Our relationship with God is vital to our ability to win the spiritual battle.

We have stressed that our enemy, although strong and dangerous, is defeated. Christ delivered the crushing blow at the cross. That doesn't mean that the enemy is not dangerous and it doesn't mean that we are not vulnerable to attack.

It is like a boxing match. In a prize fight many times the fight is decided by one blow. Rarely is a fighter knocked out by one punch but there is usually one punch that takes the strength out of the opponent's legs, that destroys his inner resolve and leads ultimately to the boxer's defeat. That telling blow was delivered at Calvary by Jesus Christ. This does not mean that the opponent is not still dangerous. If we don't keep our guard up we could be badly hurt. We need God's help, His power and resource to be strong and effective in our battle against Satan.

Remember this world is not our home. This world does not belong to us. The world is in the hands and under the sway of the evil one. You see, we live in a hostile environment. This world belongs to our enemy. He is the god of this world (2 Corinthians 4:4). He is fighting against the true God, our God. Satan is doing his best to hurt God's plan and God's creation.

This means that he is fighting against the church and against Christians. We live in the enemy's realm. If we are to succeed or even survive, we need the help and the power of God. The analogy of the Vine and the branches was not just to show our relationship to the Lord. It stressed the vital importance of staying connected to spiritual-life flow.

That is what James is stressing in this portion of scripture. Another analogy that applies is one of the old-time diving suits, where the deep sea diver is connected to the surface by an air hose and communication line. The diver can freely move about in this hostile and foreign environment because he has life support from his own world.

We, too, are in a hostile world. We are connected to God by the Holy Spirit and draw our life and our strength from Him. It is vital that we keep our connection clear and open, and that we don't get entangled in the world or break our connection.

"THEREFORE SUBMIT TO GOD"

In any war there can only be one supreme commander. He lays out the strategy. He plans the battles. He may even retreat and give up territory to get a better position. One thing is clear, in a war we must obey orders. If we can't or if we don't, we will surely lose the war. We must remember there is a larger strategy at work. We may not understand the plan but we must follow it. We must submit.

This word submit, in the Greek, means "to be obedient to." We must be obedient to God. We must be obedient to His word and to His plan for our lives and for our church. We are at war with Satan. We must follow orders or we may end up being in the wrong place at the wrong time and get into trouble. Has that ever happened to you? It happens.

It is hard for us to follow orders. We have a hard time being obedient. We live in a permissive and rebellious society. We pride ourselves on our independence and rebelliousness. Currently, the heroes of our society, the media creations, are the antisocial rebels that scorn authority. On television, the children tell the parents what to do. Teachers, supervisors, leaders, anyone in authority, are shown to be old fashioned, inflexible and usually stupid. We have been taught and are teaching our children to defy authority. Submission has become a dirty word. Yet God says "Submit."

Submission means absolute and total commitment. We must come to the place in our lives where we are fully committed to the truth that Jesus Christ is Lord. If Jesus is not our Lord, then He is not anything in our life. As our Lord, He has the right to ask us to do anything, to go anywhere, at anytime. It is our part to obey.

John in First John 2:3 says, if we know and love God we will keep His commandments. This is true for all Christians. We must fully understand Jesus is Lord.

The New Testament is full of commands on how to live. We are instructed about our walk, our relationships and about nearly every phase of our lives. Are we being obedient to God? Do we attempt to follow the Bible's teachings about life and relationships? Do we faithfully "assemble" ourselves together? If God speaks to the leadership of the church and leads them to have two different services on Sunday do we attend? Are we obedient to Christ as he speaks through His pastor or church? Are we obedient to the Lord's plan for our lives? Are we listening to what Jesus is saying to us on a daily basis?

That leads to the next instruction from James (4:7-8). James tells us how to hear from God. How we can receive God's plan for our lives and for our church. How we can learn to be obedient.

"DRAW NEAR TO GOD"

The first lesson for those who are going to enter into spiritual warfare is <u>submit</u>. The second is <u>draw near to God</u>. The message of the Bible is clear. God is looking for a people to call His people. He created man for fellowship. God would come to man in the cool of the evening and walk with him. He wants a personal relationship with us. We call Him Father for good reason. God wants a personal, heart-felt relationship with each and every believer. Unfortunately, too many of us look at Him like He is a Sugar-Daddy, who is there just to supply our needs, than like a true, loving Father who not only cares about us but whom we love.

We Draw Near Through Prayer

James says, draw near to God. How do we do it? It begins with a personal prayer life that stresses relationship and not personal need. We can't stress enough the importance of prayer. Prayer is the barometer of our spirituality and our relationship to God. Do we pray? Do we spend time in the presence of our Lord? We have stressed that prayer is not simply presenting our needs. God knows what you need. He wants us to get to know Him. We need to truly understand His character and love for us.

Our goal as Christians should be to <u>know</u> God personally. What truly transforms a believer is becoming a friend to God. When we learn how much God loves us, how he only wants the ultimate best for us, then it is easy to trust Him and even easier to believe that God will move in our behalf.

In prayer God does draw near. We become sensitive to the presence of God. God has never been far away but we fail to recognize His nearness. We are so busy we miss the best parts. Why do we spend so much time praying. As one writer said, "One day we will come knocking at heaven's gate and we want God to be able to recognize our voice." More significantly, we want to come to the place in our lives where we can recognize the voice of God. We need to spend time not just praying but listening. We can hear from God. We must hear from God.

We must recognize His voice because we need help right now. We need to hear what God is saying to us as a church and as individuals so that we can fulfill the plan of God for our lives and for ministries. We can't be obedient if we are not listening to our Lord. We can't be in our place of ministry if we are not hearing God's voice leading us to our rightful place.

How Do We Recognize His Voice?

What if we can't recognize His voice? We often ask ourselves, is that God or is it just me? Is the enemy trying to mislead us? The Bible says we can recognize the voice of the Lord. In John 10:27, Jesus said, "My sheep hear my voice, and I know them, and they follow me." There is a quality about His voice that touches our spirit. Remember, too, that the enemy and self always fall back to glorifying self and the things of the world. The Spirit of God glorifies the Lord. The more we spend time in His presence the easier is it to recognize the voice of the loving Savior.

The Key Is Prayer

The bottom line is we need to pray. Prayer is the key not only to spiritual warfare but to personal growth. The more you pray the closer to God you will feel. The closer to God you are, the stronger you will become. The stronger you become the easier it will be to win the spiritual battle.

Everybody wants to be strong and do great exploits for God. Not all do. What is the problem? Prayer. We all have so many important things to do in our lives that prayer becomes perfunctory. We begin the day with a few moments of asking God to bless our efforts and go on our way. At meals, we by rote mumble some words of grace. In the evening, we ask God to forgive us any failures just in case the Grim Reaper comes in the dead of night.

That is until we get into trouble. When the world starts caving in on us, we know how to pray. We pray and pray until we hear from God. Sometimes, trouble is the only way to get our attention and bring us back to the one who truly loves us. We all pray. The key is what is our motivation? We can't afford to wait until we have to pray. Satan will wreak havoc in your life if you wait until you have to pray.

Making Prayer Easier

Let's make it easy to pray. Set a time and place for prayer. We are told that Jesus would arise early and find a place of solitude for prayer. We should do the same. Spend uninterrupted time with God.

Just talk to God. The best times of prayer are just simple conversations with your Father in heaven. You may want to follow the pattern set in the Lord's prayer. Begin with praise, then pray for the kingdom, the Lord's will to be done, to meet our needs, to forgive us, to lead us, to protect us and give us victory over the evil one and to close with praise.

Take time to just sit quietly and listen. Bring along some paper and a pen. You may want to write down what the Lord is saying to you. Take your time. Prayer is the most important thing you will do all day. It can make or break your day. Make prayer a priority. Prayer truly makes a difference in life and in the nearness of God.

"CLEANSE YOUR HANDS AND PURIFY YOUR HEARTS"

To truly draw near, to really get close to God, to come into the Lord's presence in an intimate way, we have to change. James 4:8 states, "Cleanse your hands, purify your hearts."

Isaiah is considered to be the greatest of the Old Testament prophets. He was a man who held a high standard of personal holiness in a time of great spiritual decline. He was on intimate relations with God. He spoke God's words with boldness and assurance that came from that personal, close relationship with the Lord God.

In Isaiah chapter six, we see Isaiah coming into the presence of the Living God. Isaiah is in the throne room of God. He sees the seraphim and cherubim ministering around the exalted God. He cries out, "I am undone.." He felt unprepared to be in the presence of God. Isaiah was a sinner. He did things and said things, he didn't want to do and say.

Everyone can identify with Isaiah. We all do things, say things and think things we shouldn't. It is easy in the world we live in to find ourselves doing what we shouldn't and allowing it to become commonplace in our lives. We need to stop and allow the Holy Spirit to show us what we need to change.

Being A Holy Warrior

If we want to become strong spiritual warriors for the Lord, if we desire to draw close to God, we can't allow anything to hinder us in our desire to come near to God. Yet that is exactly what the devil tries to do. It is Satan's plan to weigh us down with sin. The devil is always trying to find the chinks in the spiritual soldier's armor. Satan wants to discover our weakness. If Satan can get us to fail he has won a great victory.

How? He wants to use personal sin and failure to make us feel unworthy to be used by God. It isn't just that we will feel unworthy, the devil uses the guilt of our failures to stop us from drawing near to God. We can almost dread coming to Him because we know that we have failed again. God doesn't condemn but our guilt does. God waits with all His love to forgive and to restore.

This is a call to personal holiness. James is saying to be prepared for spiritual battle, to withstand the enemy and to get him to flee. You must change.

It is submit, draw close and lay aside the things that would hinder you in the battle. The writer of Hebrews (12:1) says the same thing, "Lay aside every weight.." Get rid of the hindrances. When you are in a battle, in hand-to-hand combat, you only want what is truly necessary for you to win. You need your armor and your weapons but anything else will simply weigh you down and could bring you to defeat.

Again, this is important. Christian holiness is based on relationship and obedience. We have been made acceptable to God by His grace. We are worthy because of the work of Christ. Paul, in Second Corinthians (5:21), says, "For He (God the Father) made Him (Christ) who knew no sin to be sin for us, that we might become the righteousness of God in Him." It was God's work.

We maintain that righteousness through the continued work of Christ and through our obedience to the Spirit and the Word. We read the Bible, God's Word, and see how we are to live. When we do wrong the Spirit convicts and we obey.

The Word of God becomes an agent of change for us. We read the Bible or we hear the word of God preached and the Spirit speaks to our spirit about change. We see our sins, our incorrect attitudes, and we come under conviction. In obedience to the Holy Spirit, we repent and ask forgiveness of our sins. The wonderful thing we need to recognize is that the Holy Spirit not only convicts and cleanses, He is there to help us to stay free from our sins. We must stand ready to quickly obey the Spirit.

We need to keep our lives free from sin. Paul made it clear in Galatians (5:1), "Stand fast therefore in the liberty by which Christ has made us free, and do not be entangled again with the yoke of bondage." Paul is pointing back to our salvation, the work of Christ at the cross. The Lord broke the power of sin and of the enemy over us. Christ set us free from the bondage of sin. Now, as warriors, Christian soldiers on the front line, we must stand fast, be strong, unbendable in our resolve to stay free from any hindrance that would prevent us from being or doing our best.

If we are pure, undefiled in Christ, then nothing can prevent us from being victorious over the enemy. Nothing will hinder the flow of the Holy Spirit's anointing on our lives. We will draw close to God, becoming ever stronger. We will submit to the will of God. We will be sensitive to the Spirit's leading, His convicting touch and maintain a purity of heart.

Let's Get Practical.. How Then Should We Live?

How should we live? If we want to be a person who puts the enemy to flight, a person who has the anointing and the power of God working in his life then we must follow the instructions of the Word. Paul in both Colossians 3:5-24 and Ephesians 4:17-32 tells us how to live. In Ephesians, Paul says, "Put aside the works of the flesh and the ways of the world. Change your walk. Don't live like the unsaved." Paul gets quite specific. "Put away lying, stealing, evil speaking and such."

Paul doesn't stop there. He goes on to say, "Replace that way of living with a walk in the Spirit." This is significant. We get the idea that holiness is simply putting away certain things, frailties and inappropriate behaviors from our lives. No, it is not simply putting off. It is also putting on. Paul goes on to say, walk this way. Live this Way. Walk in the Spirit. How? Act this way. Be kind, tenderhearted, forgiving.

Then Paul goes on to say something really quite astounding. In Ephesians chapter five, verse one, he says, "Be imitators of God.." Act like God. Act like God acted through Christ Jesus. We are to act like God. To love like God loved Us. Paul is teaching us, under the anointing and direction of the Holy Spirit, how to have victory over sin and how we can become like Jesus. We are to replace negative behavior with positive behavior. The more we do this the stronger we will become. The easier it will be to stay free.

Remember, never forget for one moment, we are in a battle. The stakes are extremely high. The souls of men, women and children are at stake. We are fighting Satan for the control of people's lives. We must win.

We must be strong. We must fight and pull down the enemy's strongholds. We must take back that which the enemy has stolen. To accomplish these goals, to put the devil to flight, we need more of God in our lives. You don't throw a bucket of water on a blazing house and expect many results. You put as much water as you can on the fire. We must submit to God, draw near to Him and lay aside any hindrances to our becoming strong and mighty in the Lord.

CHAPTER SIX

PUT ON THE RIGHT ARMOR

The Devil has one goal in dealing with humankind. He wants to keep the unsaved blind to the truth of the gospel and he wants to keep Christians as miserable as possible. Why? When Christians are miserable they turn their thoughts and actions inward. They get concerned about themselves. Instead of fighting the fight of faith, they get caught up in the "I need, I want" syndrome. When we are thinking about ourselves, we spend very little time praying and ministering to others.

Let us have a clear understanding of this truth. Remember Jesus said, in John 10:10, that the evil one has come to steal, kill and destroy. The devil wants to steal your peace. He wants to kill your faith.

He wants to destroy your effectiveness. If you are a believer, the devil wants to keep you discouraged, depressed and downhearted.

Think about this. If Satan can get us all caught up in worrying about ourselves, if he can get us concerned about how we are going to survive, then he is not going to have to worry about us as opponents. As a matter of fact, he might even be able to use us to help keep others ineffective, too. Don't you know that Satan uses good people to keep other good people under control.

How are we used by the devil? When we are negative, when we speak words of discouragement, the moment we open our mouth to complain. When we start telling others what they are doing wrong. When we start saying the word "can't" a lot. The times we start to condemn others or criticize. Satan loves that. See, we can be used to destroy the faith of others.

Another way we are used by the devil is by being apathetic. When we get the old blahs and we just sit around doing nothing. The old devil really enjoys that. He roars with laughter when believers act faith-less or just get to the place of not doing anything at all.

As believers, we need to wake up. Remember we are at war. We have to learn to recognize the influences of the evil one. What should we do? We must keep ourselves ready for any attack. The enemy is con-stantly going around looking for the opportunity to get a claw-hold in our lives. He searches for the weak and for the unaware. We cannot afford to allow the enemy any opening. That is why Paul warns us in Ephesians, "Stand, Put on the whole armor of God..". Be ready for the attack and you can win the battle.

WHAT IS THE ARMOR OF GOD?

In the book of Ephesians, Paul deals with the spiritual war. In Ephesians 6: 14-17, Paul not only describes the warfare but points to our preparation. Paul is saying we must be prepared for the enemy's attack. We need to be ready for the fiery darts and the sneak attacks. Paul says, "Christian, Take a stand. Put on the armor. Get ready to fight."

The language here is obviously symbolic. He is talking about a warfare and a preparation that is not seen by the human eye. Even in the description, Paul gives us the spiritual applications of the armor. He speaks of being girded about with "truth", having put on the breastplate of "righteousness", having our feet shod with the "preparation of the gospel of peace."

Do not miss this. The emphasis here is the warfare. Paul is using the analogy of the soldier's armor because we are in a spiritual battle and we must be spiritually prepared. Over and over Paul says, "put on" the armor. That means we have a real choice. We can put on the armor and be prepared or we can ignore the commands and be ill-prepared for the coming warfare.

As people under the authority of Christ, we must put on the armor. We must fight and win.

Put On The Whole Armor Of God

Don't miss the emphasis placed by Paul on putting on the WHOLE armor of God. Twice in three verses Paul points to putting on the whole armor. Certainly, Paul is saying you can't go to war half-prepared. You'll lose.

It is almost humorous seeing some soldier scampering toward the fight. The soldier is hopping on one foot trying to get his other sandal on. His helmet is jammed on the back of his head. The breastplate is half on, hanging by one strap. Under his arm, pressed against his side, is his sword. In his other hand he carries, no drags, his shield. Funny until you consider the consequences. We can't wait until we hear the battle trumpets to start putting on our armor. We must be ready for the battle. We must have our armor on and sword in hand.

There is more to this command. We must realize that we have been given ALL the armor. Christ gave us what we need at the cross. Christ not only disarmed the enemy at the cross (Colossians 2:15), He made provision for us to fight the fight of faith. The armor Paul describes points to the work of Christ in us. We don't have to earn the armor or grow into it. The armor has been provided by our Lord.

Paul writes of being "girded" with "truth." We received the truth, when we received Christ. It is Jesus Christ, who is the Way, "The Truth" and The Life (John 14:6). When we accepted Jesus as our Lord and Savior, we appropriated righteousness through Christ's work at the cross.. Remember, Paul told us in Second Corinthians 5:21, Jesus became sin for us that we might become the "righteousness" of God.

When we became believers we received Jesus Christ. As Paul says, in Romans (13:14), we put on the Lord Jesus Christ. Paul is saying, we died to the old man and now we live for Christ. We no longer act as we used to act. We are not controlled by our flesh but we obey the leading of Christ.

When we are in Christ we become like Him. We begin to appropriate His nature, His character. When we put on the armor we are laying hold of, acknowledging and accepting the work that Christ did for us. We are receiving that which the Lord has provided for us. Why does Paul say "put on" the armor, if we have already received it?

The problem is that we don't accept what Christ has done for us. We many times fail to accept that we are the righteousness of God. We look at ourselves and we know that we still fail God. We sin. We can't accept the fact that we have been made righteous not by our works or our lives but the singular work of Christ at the cross. That is not how our logical minds work. The work has been done. The armor has been provided. It sits before us. Paul says, "Put it on."

We must pick up the armor. We must accept what Christ has provided and put it on. Knowing that we stand not on what our flesh thinks but on what Christ has declared through His holy Word.

The Distinctive Language Used By Paul

Look at the tense used by Paul in describing the first few pieces of armor. In Ephesians 6:14-15, "Stand therefore, <u>having girded</u> your waist with truth, <u>having put</u> on the breastplate of righteousness, <u>having shod</u> your feet with the preparation of the gospel of peace;" Paul is writing in the past tense. That is significant. Paul is pointing to the fact that we already have this armor. The key word is "<u>having</u>."

This is the armor we have obtained through Christ's work on the cross of Calvary. We as believers have immediately received these pieces of armor. We need to accept and believe that we have these things as part of the work of salvation. We must believe that we have them. God said it. When God says something we do believe it, don't we?

THE FIRST THREE PIECES OF ARMOR

Having Girded Your Loins With Truth

Look at the first piece of armor. Having "Girded" your loins with truth. Girded is a rather strange word. We translate this word to mean "girdle." The word refers to a leather garment that was used to hold the tunic out of the way. When a soldier would go out to battle, he would not want anything to encumber his freedom of movement. He would take the loose part of his tunic or cape and tuck it into the girdle. He then would have the freedom to move any way he would choose without getting tripped up by his own garments.

When Satan attacks he tries to undermine our faith. He wants to trip us up. The old enemy comes along and begins to whisper his insidious lies. "You can't make it. God won't answer your prayers. How could God love you after what you have done. You have failed God and He has given up on you. God doesn't care." It is a **LIE**.

We must gird ourselves with the truth. Know this great truth before all others. Jesus Christ is Lord. He is God and reigns omnipotent. Jesus has shown His great and unending love for you by taking your place on the cross. We did nothing to earn that love and we can do nothing to change it. The complete and unalterable truth is God LOVES us. This truth should change us. It must change the way we think, act and feel. It doesn't matter what our old flesh thinks. God has said He loves us and He proved it through his Son.

We are going to make it. No matter what we face. We will not only survive, we will win. In our times of troubles, in the struggles of life, in the spiritual battles, we can know that God is with us. Jesus said He would be with us until the very end (Matthew 28:20). He will hear your prayers and He will answer. We can and should WIN at life.

The Lord has given us everything we need to win. The truth is that our Lord Jesus Christ is the Lord of all creation. Jesus has made provision for us. In Luke chapter ten, Jesus had sent out His disciples to do His work. When they returned they were rejoicing over the miracles they had seen. They remarked how they even had authority over evil spirits. Jesus tells them how He, in the Spirit, has seen Satan falling from heaven like lightning. Jesus is declaring that this is only the beginning of what the enemy will suffer at the hands of the Lord and His church. Jesus then describes the power and authority that He provides for His followers.

Jesus told them, in Luke 10:19, "Behold, I give you the <u>authority</u> to trample on serpents and scorpions, and over all power of the enemy, and nothing shall by any means hurt you." Jesus has given us the power and the authority to defeat the devil and his minions. We have this authority because we act in His Name, and His Power because we have received the Spirit of God to do what He wills for our lives.

When we are under attack, when the enemy seems like he will overwhelm us, when the forces of darkness come whispering that you have no chance and God won't help, stand. Stand on these truths. Remember who you are, Whom you serve and what God has promised. It is the answer to the great question. In struggle we always ask, "Why?" When that question comes up, remember the first letter "W". That should remind us of the four "W"s. Who am I? Whom do I serve? What has He promised? **We Win!**

We should tell ourselves, "I am a child of God. The Lord God, Who rules over all creation including all spiritual beings, is my God. He has given me power and authority to defeat all power of the enemy. He is with me. I will win."

We have the truth on our side. We must learn to always go **back** to the truth. We cannot rely on what we think, feel or are told. There are times when we think wrong. There are times when our feelings lead us astray. There are times when the things we are told are in error. We must stand on the truth. The truth is what we have been given by the Lord.

Having Put On The Breastplate Of Righteousness

This is so important. Too many Christians struggle with feelings of unworthiness. It happens to every believer. We are so aware of our own shortcomings. We know our every fault. We know when we sin. We know that even when we do our best we still fail. We say the wrong thing. We do the wrong thing. We think the wrong thing. We struggle with our sins. That is good.

The difference between a Christian and a non-Christian is not that the Christian doesn't sin. The Bible says we all sin. The non-believer doesn't care if he sins. The non-Christian many times can't wait to sin. They will tell you they can't wait until Friday night or whenever to go out and sin. When they do sin, sometimes there is a prick of conscience, but for the most part they don't care. Christians, on the other hand, hate their sins. They get sick over their sins. They want to do their best for their Lord. That's good. The Lord can use that to bring about change and help us to overcome the sins that ensnare us.

That has nothing to do with our standing before God. Our right standing before God is through Jesus Christ and Jesus Christ alone. Remember what Paul said, in Second Corinthians (5:21), Jesus became sin for us, that we might become the righteousness of God.

What did we do to earn salvation? Nothing. Did we ever think that we had to do something? Yes. Most people believe that they have to clean themselves up to become Christians. They will say things like, "when I quit drinking, smoking, or whatever then I will come to church and become a Christian." We were wrong. It was the work of Christ on the cross that made us acceptable to God and our salvation is based on God's work alone. We can't please God by our own efforts. We must trust in God and God alone. Then why do we try to please God through our own efforts after we are saved?

In Romans chapter eight, verse one, we are told, "There is therefore now no condemnation to those who are in Christ Jesus." That verse ends right there in the most reliable manuscripts. Why now? It is because the Lord has paid for our sins on the cross. The penalty was paid for all sins. The sins we have committed in the past and the sins we now commit. The price was fully paid. All we have to do is put them on the cross. Doesn't that give the license to sin? No! We try not to sin, **not** because of the law or the penalty of the law. We try NOT to sin because we love our Lord and Savior.

We must remember the truth: God loves us. He loves us with a "perfect" love (I John 4:18). If God loves us with a perfect love can God love us any more? No. If God loves us with a perfect love can he love us any less? No. What if we fail? What if we sin? Does God love any less? **No.**

We are praying and seeking God. See the scene in heaven. Satan stands before the throne of God. Satan is accusing us of our "unworthy" behavior. He screams, "They are no good. They have sinned. They have failed you over and over again. Don't answer their prayers." Satan is totally correct. We are all that he says and more. Then Jesus steps to the judgment bar, "Yes, they have failed, Father, but they are one of mine." Case Closed. Satan howls. He has lost. There is **No** condemnation.

We need to realize that we are worthy. Say that, "I am worthy." Say it again and again. We are worthy. We are worthy because Jesus Christ has made us worthy. Don't listen to self, the world or the enemy. When you hear that horrible, slanderous lie, "God is angry with you. God is disappointed. God has turned His back because.." Say, "No, that is a **Lie**."

Paul, in Romans chapter eight, asks, "Who can separate us from the love of God?" The answer is simple. No one and nothing can. I am worthy because Christ has made me worthy.

The "Popeye" Verse

Every Christian needs to learn the "Popeye" verse. It makes us strong. It is better than spinach. See, anyone can get discouraged. Even Paul got discouraged. In First Corinthians chapter fifteen, Paul is speaking of the resurrection. Paul goes through the list of those who have seen the crucified Jesus alive. He comes to his own witness. In verse nine, he describes himself, as the least of the apostles. He says, "I am.. not worthy to be called an apostle, because I persecuted the church." Paul is saying my past makes me unworthy. Do you ever feel that way?

Look at verse ten, "But by the grace of God.. 'I am what I am,' and His grace toward me was not in vain.." Paul is saying, God knows me, He knows what I am. He knows my frailties, my weaknesses. He knows my past and my future. God knows that I am flesh and He still chose me. God's grace was not in vain. He knew exactly when and where I will fail and He still loves and uses me.

God knows who we are. God knows our every weakness. In Psalm 103:14, the Psalmist says, "For He (The Lord) knows our frame, He remembers that we are dust." We are what we are. We are flesh. God knows you are flesh and blood. He knows what makes up our character and heart. He knows all of our past sins and our future ones. He still chose us.

God does not turn His back on us because we fail. As with Peter, when Peter denied Him, the Lord was there to restore. When we fall, He is there to pick us up, to get us back on our feet and to lead us on. He loves us. Satan wants to convince us that God is disappointed with us and has given up on us. It is a **Lie.**

"I am what I am.." This doesn't mean we aren't changing. We are constantly being perfected by the Holy Spirit. What it means is that the Lord knew we where flesh and blood, fully capable of failing, when He chose us. It means that failure is part of being human, that our failures mean that we have room for growth.

The Lord doesn't expect perfection from us. He expects us to have hearts that want to do our best and try our hardest to love and obey him. But as long as we are in the world and in the flesh, He knows that we will sin. He is there to help us to win over sin, to get us back on our feet and going forward.

Know this, God loves you and is more willing to forgive than we are to ask for forgiveness. He wants you to immediately return to the battles and let the enemy know that he hasn't defeated you. We are righteous, worthy to be used by the Lord.

So when you are in the heat of the battle and the enemy throws you a fiery dart, even if it hits and we fail our God, the wound is not fatal, our heart is protected by the Breastplate of Righteousness. It is a breastplate forged at the cross and well capable of protecting our spiritual life. It is a breastplate that allows us to declare our righteousness, not in ourselves or acts or deeds, but our righteousness in Christ Jesus, our mighty Lord and Savior.

Having Shod Your Feet With The Preparation Of The Gospel Of Peace

The success of the Roman Army has been credited to great leadership, better organization and a hundred other things. One thing that the Roman soldier had that others lacked was a uniform. The Roman soldier was fully equipped for war from the top of his head to the bottom of his feet. The Roman soldier wore sandals that were made for war. The sandal was leather and had a sole that allowed for standing in places where others would slip. In a fierce battle, in the rocky terrain, being able to stand and move freely without losing your footing made the difference in many battles.

Paul is declaring that the Christian Soldier in the spiritual battle has to make a stand. You need firm footing if you are going to stand your ground. You need a solid foundation. Paul says that solid footing is the gospel of peace.

Mark this down. To be ready to fight and win, we must have peace in our hearts. We must come to the place where we know that God's hand is on our lives. We stand in faith. Not in blind faith but a faith that has been birthed through the truth of the gospel. We stand on truths that have been tested and tried for two thousand years. Truths and teachings that have been spelled out in the word of God, the Bible.

We know that God is the only true God. We know that God loves us. He has manifested, shown us, that love through His Son, Jesus Christ. God has a plan for this world and for our lives. He is working His will through us even now. When we are in the battle, we can know that He is with us and that He has empowered us to win.

In a battle, there is nothing worse than fear. Strong armies have lost many battles and wars because of fear. Fear can cause strong men to turn and run from certain victory. Fear cannot have a place in the battle.

One of Satan's greatest weapons is fear. He goes about LIKE a roaring lion. The lion roars to generate fear, to put the prey on the move, to frighten the victim into racing near the hiding pride of lions. It is a tactic designed to bring the prey down to certain death and defeat.

We must have it settled in our hearts. Satan has no power over us. Our God is mighty and we will win. We enter the battle knowing that God is with us. Like David, we remind ourselves, no matter how great the foes seem to be, our God is mightier. We know that this battle is not ours alone, but that it ultimately belongs to the Lord. We go into battle with sure footing, with peace, standing on the promises of the word of God.

PUT ON THE RIGHT ARMOR

We need to be people of the Word. We should know the promises of God. As we read the Bible we are changed. We begin to see and understand our position in Christ. We read about the many times that the Lord moved in behalf of His people and our faith grows. When the battle comes our hearts are filled with knowledge and faith. We have peace. We are ready for the battle.

There is more. We need to be people of good morale. To be strong in the Lord and to encourage others in the battle, we need to be positive and uplifting. We need to speak words of victory. Anybody can complain. Anyone can speak words of discouragement, especially, in times of war and struggle.

Paul said, "Stand.." This is an image of a soldier standing tall, his armor glistening in the sunlight, his cape blowing in the breeze, helmet down on his brow, a look of determination is on his face. He stands with his sword at the ready. He is a strong and ready warrior waiting to hear the battle trumpet. The look on his face says it all. He is ready for war. He is sure in the knowledge that he and his forces will win. He is strong in the Lord.

Are You Ready For The Battle?

There is the armor. There is the leather girdle, the breastplate and the sandals. They have been prepared for you. They were purchased at a great price. Listen to Paul, hear his words, as he speaks in the anointing of the Holy Spirit, "Stand.. Having put on the armor.." We must accept what God has done for us. We must stand on the truth. We must know that we are righteous in God's eyes. We must have the assurance that God's word is true and that we will win the battle.

God has not called us to the spiritual battle to lose. He has called us to this struggle to WIN. Don't be afraid to enter the fray. Don't be concerned about the power of the enemy. We serve a mighty God, who has planned many victories for us. We will Win.

CHAPTER SEVEN

Watch Out For Fiery Darts

The army is called to the front. The soldiers find themselves in hand-to-hand battle with the enemy. The bullets are flying, bombs are bursting, men are locked in life and death struggles. One soldier runs to his sergeant, panic is written on his face.

The soldier cries out, "Sarge, they are shooting at me. These guys want to kill me. I didn't join the army for this. I joined the army because I liked the uniform. I get excited when I see the brass bands and the flags waving. I liked the parades but I don't like the fighting."

Armies are not formed for parades, for flag waving, for show. Armies are formed for one reason. War. We may call them peacekeepers or a thousand other socially acceptable names but armies are for war.

Christians sometimes forget that life is a war. We are on the front lines. The enemy is attacking us. Life becomes a struggle and we get upset. We start to complain. We get all caught up in self-pity.

Actually, we are praising the devil for his success against us. We begin to express to others and ourselves how Satan is winning the battle against us. Now the Bible says, give thanks in everything, but that means thanks to God not to the devil.

We act surprised when we come under attack. Why? We should express surprise when we are not being fought by the devil. We begin to doubt our worthiness. We look for reasons why we are in the struggle. We begin to wonder what did we do or say to bring this calamity on.

We are in a WAR. Satan wants to defeat you. He wants to destroy your witness. He wants to make your ministry of no effect. We must refuse to allow him any victories in our lives. How? There is only one way. Put on your armor and fight back.

WHEN ATTACKED.. PUT ON THE WHOLE ARMOR

We have seen that we must be ready. We need to have our armor on when the battle comes. We have no time to stop and put on the armor when the attack comes. We must put on the whole armor and be ready to fight.

In the last chapter we looked at the girdle, the breastplate and the sandals. Paul spoke of these in the past tense. He showed us how these pieces of armor, representing various spiritual truths, were provided by our Lord Jesus at the cross. Paul kept saying "having" put on.

Paul changes his commands in dealing with the shield and the helmet. Paul says, "Taking the shield.." and "Take the helmet". Paul uses action verbs. We are required to act. Paul is saying take your shield, take your helmet, take your sword. We are required to act. We are required to defend ourselves. Christ has provided but now we are to take an active part in the battle. We must do something.

Taking The Shield Of Faith To Quench The Fiery Darts

As Christians, we believe the Bible. We have made Jesus Christ our Lord And Savior. That means if Jesus tells us in His Word to do something then we should do it. If Jesus tells us something we should believe it. In the Bible the Lord through Paul tells us we are righteous. Then we must be righteous. Jesus tells us that He will see us through every struggle, every battle and the hard places of life. Then He will do it. Remember, He stands before us with a sword in His Hand, ready to do battle. We cannot lose. Do we believe it?

Paul says, "taking up the shield of **Faith..**" We have to take up the shield of faith if we are going to fight the enemy and win. What is faith? Faith is.. There are a thousand definitions of faith. Let's make it easy. Faith is simply acting on belief.

This faith Paul is speaking of is not simply Christianity. We say we are part of The Faith. We can say that because there is really only one word for faith. Paul is not saying pick up the shield of salvation or belief. He is writing to believers. Paul is saying, if you are going to quench the fiery darts of the enemy, you must believe what God has said and act on it. This faith is believing and acting on what the Lord has said.

To understand this, let's look at the fiery darts. These fiery darts have a source. Paul says they are from the wicked one. Who is this wicked one? It is none other than Satan. These fiery darts are satanic attacks. Satan comes along and attacks the believer. He uses a lot of fiery darts. He tries to undermine our faith. If that doesn't work, he tries to makes us feel unworthy to be used by God. He then tries to convince us that we cannot possibly succeed.

Do you know what Satan's favorite weapon is against believers? Mark this down, remember it. It is **Wrong Thinking**. The real battlefield for the believer is the mind. Listen to Paul in Second Corinthians 10:3-5. He begins by reminding us our warfare is not in the flesh. He goes on to say, our weapons are not "carnal" but spiritual, for the pulling down of strongholds. What kind of strongholds?

Listen to verse five, "Casting down arguments and every high thing that exalts itself against the knowledge of God, bringing every **Thought** into captivity to the obedience of Christ."

Where does the believer keep his knowledge of God? Where are our thoughts? See the battleground is in the mind of the individual believer. We have to get our thinking right. Before we can defeat the enemy in the world, we must win the battle of the mind. We must tear down the stronghold of wrong thinking.

We think like the rest of the world. We find ourselves exalting the knowledge of science or philosophy or the false teachings of Satan and then wonder why we struggle.

Sometimes, we think like we have already lost. We expect defeat. Something bad happens and we say something like, "Oh, I knew that would happen." We make a mistake and we tell ourselves, "Oh how dumb of me, how stupid." We, too often, start off saying, "I can't.." We are ruled by doubt and fear.

The enemy uses **fear,** **doubt** and **condemnation** to control Christians, to keep us in the bondage of ineffectiveness, so that we as Christians are afraid to try or are defeated before we start. Remember, Jesus warned us about the evil one. He said, the evil one has come to kill, steal and destroy. He wants to keep believers miserable and defeated.

Doubts are not even Christian. We can't afford to doubt. We are children of God. We are to have faith. We are to believe the word of God and act on it. We are not stupid or dumb. God didn't make us stupid or dumb. God has given us wisdom through His Son Jesus Christ. He is with us to bring forth His glory in our lives and we don't have to be afraid or concerned. Don't doubt, have faith. When the wicked one attacks us, if we are going to win, we must have faith.

Quenching The Fiery Darts..

Let's get practical. How do we use our faith to quench the fiery darts? Paul says quench. Quench here simply means to extinguish. When the devil shoots a fiery arrow at our home, we must put out the fire. Well, how do we do it?

First, when wrong thinking arises recognize the source. We are new creatures in Christ Jesus. We have been given the Holy Spirit to rule over our lives and our minds. If our thoughts are not in line with the teachings of Christ, if they are condemning us, if they are full of doubts and fear, they are not from God nor have they been produced by your spiritual nature. So reject them.

Listen, this is important, we must say to ourselves, "I reject these thoughts; they are not from God or honoring to him." Why do that? We are accomplishing two things. One, we are openly rejecting the work of the devil and our old nature. Two, we are building our faith by establishing a pattern of dealing with wrong thinking. We are, in effect, taking up the shield of faith and quenching the fiery darts.

Secondly, we must recognize that the enemy is persistent. Some wrong thinking becomes ingrained in our thought processes. We must stand on James 4:7, "Resist the devil and he will flee." We must train ourselves to resist wrong thinking. We need to consider what we are thinking and determine what is the source of that thinking? We need to consider every thought. If that thought does not line up with the teaching of God, then reject it.

It is the same thing when we feel down. We should stop and remember we are the victors. Refuse to act like an atheist, like an unbeliever who doesn't know God or His promises. When we are in a rough battle, when things aren't going exactly as we want, when we get afraid, remember, we have God with us. We will win. We pick up our shield of faith. We remember what God has told us in His word. We should be able to tell the enemy, Jesus said..

This requires us to be people of the word. We can't act on the word of God unless we know what it says. We need to study and read and put the word of God in our hearts if we are going to believe what it says and act on it. That leads right to the next piece of armor we must take up.

TAKE UP THE HELMET OF SALVATION

The Roman soldier would carry his helmet. It was the last piece of armor he would put on. The Roman helmet of leather and metal banded together was cumbersome and hot. It was necessary because the head became the primary target in battle.

Paul says, take up the helmet of salvation. This salvation was not the saving of the soul. Paul was writing to believers. He was speaking of a different kind of salvation. Paul has been dealing with spiritual warfare. He is teaching believers about how to win the battle with the enemy. Let's look at a battle.

The Roman helmet was unique. It didn't allow for much peripheral vision. The Roman soldier would have to fix his gaze on a distant point and begin to advance. The Roman army was like a precision machine compared to most of their opponents. They would march forward, eyes fixed ahead, knowing that their fellow soldiers stood beside them and behind them. They would go forward crushing any enemy that was in front of them. They would not stop until they reached their objective.

We have an objective. Paul is reminding the believers of their objective. It is to be our foremost thought. Paul here is referring to our future salvation. In First Thessalonians chapter five, Paul speaks of the helmet, in the context of the Great Day of the Lord. In verse two, Paul says, that the Day of The Lord will come like a thief in the night. He goes on to tell believers to be prepared. In verse eight, Paul says, "Putting on the breastplate of faith and love, and as a helmet the hope of our salvation." The helmet refers to the hope of our salvation. Not the salvation of the soul but the salvation that represents the church being saved out of the world. It is a knowledge, a certain expectation that one day we will spend all of eternity with Christ.

Like the Roman Soldier, we must have our eyes fixed on our goal. Our goal is to spend eternity with God. This world is temporary at best. We can't afford to get distracted by the things of this world. It isn't that we are unconcerned about the evil that exists. We are not only concerned, we are doing something about it. It is that we refuse to allow anything to distract from our goals. We are going to fight and win. We will not allow ourselves to get caught up in the pettiness of life. We have bigger plans.

WE SHOULD BUILD OUR LIVES ON THIS KNOWLEDGE

God Has A Plan For Creation And For Us.

One, God has a plan for our lives and for this world. We are part of God's great and wondrous plan of reconciliation for all creation. God is in complete control. Sometimes, people get the idea that creation and life in general are in complete disorder. It is simply one big mess. Christians can feel that way, too, especially, when we see Satan reeking havoc in this age. It just isn't true. There is another reality.

In the Old Testament, Jeremiah the prophet, speaks to God's people. The nation of Israel was facing a critical time in its history. The people must have of thought that the world was in a mess. There was no hope and no future.

110

Jeremiah comes with a message from God. It is found in Jeremiah 29:11, God says, "I know the thoughts that I think toward you, says the Lord, thoughts of peace and not evil, to give you a future and a hope." God was saying, I have everything in control. I have a plan. It has a course to run but it will bring forth peace not evil.

In Ephesians chapter two, verse ten, the Lord says the same thing to His church. He says, "For we are His workmanship, created in Christ Jesus for **Good Works**."

God has a plan and it is at work right now. He knows exactly where we are and what we are doing. He wants the very best for us. God's plan is coming together. There are no delays. The things we are praying about and the things we long to see happen are coming to pass. Remember this there is a **Bigger Goal**. God has a plan for us and for Creation. Stand on that truth. Put on the helmet.

God Knows You And He Will Direct Your Path

The second thing we must remember is that we are part of God's plan. God **Knows** us. He directs our path. One of the simplest verses in the Bible is one of the most important for the believer in the spiritual war.

In Matthew 10:30, Jesus says, speaking of the love and care of our Father in Heaven, "But the very hairs of your head are ALL numbered." God KNOWS us. He follows our every movement. He is intimately interested in us and our well-being. He knows our needs and our wants. He loves us and wants to bless us.

God doesn't make mistakes or mess up. He really knows what He is doing. He is bringing to pass in your life the best of possible lives you could lead.

Proverbs 3:6 states, "In all your ways acknowledge Him, and He shall direct your paths." He directs the paths of the righteous. He guides us. He will lead us. We have to listen and obey. If we do, then we can miss a lot of the problems of life. We can miss some of the snares, the traps laid by the enemy. God has a plan. We are part of it. We may not fully understand. We don't have to understand. We just have to trust God and follow His directions.

Think about this for a moment. We are part of the great plans of God. God is bringing forth a wonderful new creation of beauty and awe. We have a part in that. We are now part of the great cosmic struggle. We play a part in the strategy of God. If we do our part we shall share in the rewards of the victory. We shall have the pleasure of standing before our God, knowing that we have helped bring forth good out of evil. We shall know that we helped save lives for eternity.

Our helmet is the sure knowledge of who we are in Christ and where we are going. This is the secret of life. **The Secret of Life** is knowing who you are and where you are going. We have our eyes fixed on a heavenly goal and we know that God is in complete control. We know that the Lord has a plan for us and for creation. We will not be afraid nor shall we turn aside. We know who we are in Christ and we know that we are on our way to heaven.

What we do in this spiritual battle has eternal implications. We aren't just singing songs. Praying empty words to a powerless God. We are changing creation through the anointing of the Holy Spirit. We must do our part.

CHAPTER EIGHT

HOW TO USE YOUR SWORD

Paul in Ephesians chapter six has been speaking of the spiritual armor that the believer must wear if we are to be able to stand and defeat the enemy. In verse seventeen, Paul goes on to say to take up "..the sword of the Spirit, which is the Word of God." We have a weapon to use against spiritual darkness.

If we want devils to tremble at the mention of our names, then we must take up our swords. We must become people of the Word. If we are to be a part of this war, we must do more than just stand. We must fight. We must stand up and put the enemy to flight through the use of our spiritual weapons.

We have the ultimate example of spiritual warfare. When Jesus began His ministry, He went out into the wilderness to pray. The enemy came to somehow turn Jesus aside from His mission. Satan did his best to defeat the Lord but Jesus won the battle. How? He used the Word of God. We must be people of the Word. The Bible is a powerful resource in the hands of an anointed believer.

Let's get this straight. Sometimes, people carry the Bible like it was a talisman or a good-luck charm. The Bible is just a book. It is paper and ink. What makes this Bible powerful is what it says. We must put this word to work in our lives. This book tells how to live, how to please God and how to win over the power of the enemy. It is a sword but it must be used not just carried around for an ornament to our uniform.

THE SWORDSMAN'S PREPARATION

First, Be A Believer

The first thing we need to recognize is that if we are going to stand up to the devil and win the battle, we had better know Jesus Christ as our Lord and Savior. If you are going to defeat the devil.. You must be a believer. Some have the idea that if they say the right words or use some ritual they can overcome the forces of Satan. That is simply not true.

There is the rather obvious example found in Acts (19:14), where the seven sons of the Jewish chief priest, Sceva, try to act like Paul and cast the demons out of a possessed man. The demons attacked the exorcists and put them to flight, beaten and half naked.

There is more to this than just being a Christian. We must be believers. There are Christians and there are Christians. If we are going to fight the fight, then we must not only be "In Christ" but we must believe that we can fight and win. There are too many Christians who are simply filling pews, half-heartedly doing their duty and just hanging on untill they get to heaven. We have ministers who don't even believe in the devil much less teach that we fight against him. No wonder the devil is having such success in our God-fearing nations.

Jesus said, "Follow Me.." Imitate me, become like me and greater works you will do. We are to become like Jesus. We are to be people who truly represent Christ to the world. We need to go back to the Bible and rediscover who Jesus was and what He did. Paul told the churches to become imitators of Him. He was saying act like me and you will have impact on the world and eternity.

Be A Bible Believer.. A Person Of The Word

Well, how do we do it? As believers, we become like Jesus through the Word of God. In Colossians chapter three, Paul is telling the church that we have to change. In the first part of the chapter he teaches us to leave our old ways behind. In verse twelve, Paul says we are to live differently. Put on the new man. Act like this. "Put on tender mercies, kindness, humility, meekness, long suffering; bearing with one another, and forgiving one another.. even as Christ forgave you.." Act like Christ.

Then Paul goes on to say how to do it. In verse fifteen, "Let the word of Christ dwell in you richly in all wisdom.." Get into the Word of God. Study the

Word. Paul says that the Word teaches, admonishes and corrects. As we read the Word, we are changed. We begin to see the things that need to be changed and come under conviction and try to change. We grow. We are preparing ourselves. We are getting ready for war.

We are being <u>transformed</u> into the image of Christ. We are being changed. Paul, in Second Corinthians 3:18, tells us, we are being transformed into the image of Christ. The Word of God is like a mirror. We read the Word and we see ourselves.

Sometimes, we read and we realize that we are not doing what we should be doing. The Holy Spirit convicts us. We seek God's forgiveness and commit in our hearts to try not to fail in that area again. The Holy Spirit used the Word to change us. To make us more like Jesus. We are being transformed and not just transformed but also we are strengthened.

The Word, also, builds our faith. We read about those who have gone before us. How God used men and women just like us. We read of their exploits for the Lord. We see their struggles and the victories.

Then our faith grows and we can believe that God can move through us in the same way.

The more we become like Jesus, the stronger in the faith we get, the better able we are to stand, fight and win over the enemy. There is an empowerment that comes through the handling of this sword. We are prepared by our using it. Made ready to carry it into battle and put the enemy to flight.

HOW DID JESUS FIGHT THE DIRECT ATTACK OF SATAN?

God is doing a work in the lives of Christians. He is transforming them into the image of Christ Jesus. We are to be like Christ, both in our daily lives and in our conduct as soldiers in the spiritual war. How should we fight this fight? We have a great example of how Jesus withstood the attacks of Satan. The temptation of Christ in the wilderness is documented in the book of Luke, chapter four, verses one to thirteen.

Be Filled With The Holy Spirit

In verse one, Luke is careful to note that Jesus did not go out to do battle in His own strength. Verse one clearly states, "Then Jesus being filled with the Holy Spirit returned from the Jordan and was led by the Spirit into the wilderness."

This is significant for several reasons. One, Jesus did not do anything of His own power. Paul says. in Philippians chapter two, that Jesus emptied himself of His glory and power. He was still God. He did not change His nature, but that nature did not empower Him to resist sin or work miracles. Jesus was the example to us that we, too, could resist sin and that we, too, could do ministry. Do ministry not in our own strengths but through the anointing of the Holy Spirit.

Jesus being filled with the Holy Spirit was led by the Spirit out into the wilderness to be confronted by the Satan. That should speak to us. If we are going to confront the enemy, we, too, need to be filled with the Holy Spirit. This is one of those keys to successful Christian living we need to put into our hearts. Over and over again, we are told to stay full of the Spirit. One reason we have so many problems, we run around with a near empty tank. We don't stay full.

It is the old story of the man who was in and out of church. Every few months, he would come back to church and end up at the altar during prayer meeting. Somewhere during the prayer time, he would call out to God, "O Lord, fill your servant once again with that Spirit." After a year or two of this, one old Grandma of the church got tired of it. When He cried out, "O Lord, fill your servant." She cried out, "Don't do it Lord.. he leaks."

The reality is that we all leak. We need to be full. Paul is succinct, in Ephesians 4:18, "..be filled with the Spirit," Then he goes on to tell us how to be filled, "speaking to one another in psalms and hymns and spiritual songs, singing and making melody in your heart to the Lord." He is saying, do you want to stay full? Then worship the Lord.

We all need to stop and occasionally check our spiritual gauge. We never know when we are going to be confronted by the enemy and we need to be on "full." You are not going to win the battle running on empty or a half or even three quarters. We need to be full of the Holy Spirit. We can't wait until the crisis is on us. It will be too late. We need to stay full of the Holy Spirit to win the battle.

JESUS' BATTLE WITH SATAN

Why Did Satan Tempt Jesus?

Jesus was full of the Holy Spirit. The Spirit led into the wilderness. Soon here came Satan to try to tempt Jesus to turn away from God's plan. Was Jesus sinless when he went into the wilderness? Did Jesus somehow fail God? Was it a mistake for Jesus to fast and be filled with the Spirit?

These may seem like silly questions and they are, but this is important to remember. Why do we ask ourselves the same questions when we come under attack? We come under attack and immediately we begin to question our faith, our motives, we wonder where or what we did wrong. Satan attacks believers.

Remember that. Satan attacks believers. The devil and his forces come against those who are doing their best. It is the very time when we are in the will of God, doing our very best for him that we come under attack.

Temptation Is An Attack

Luke is careful to record both Satan's attack and the Lord's replies. Satan begins with an attack on the "flesh" of Jesus. Satan appeals to the fleshly desires of hunger and pride. It is, "If you are the Son of God then turn these stones to bread."

When that doesn't work the devil comes back with an attack of materialism, worldliness, saying, look what you can have and without any effort, just worship me and I'll give you all the kingdoms of the world.

Notice that Jesus used the Word of God to answer each of Satan's attacks. Jesus was using the word to defend himself from the attacks of the devil.

Satan Uses The Word, Too.

Then came the most devilish of the temptations. It is important to see that Satan uses the Word, too. This is one of Satan's favorite tactics. He does it over and over again. Go back to the book of Genesis, back to the fall of man. You can almost hear him, "God did not say you would 'surely' die." Satan comes to Jesus quoting the Word of God.

Satan takes the Word of God out of context, he twists it, he tries to change the meaning or the intent of the word to confuse and defeat the Christian. See why we need to know what the Word of God says. When someone comes quoting scripture and we are not sure about them or what they are saying, then we should re-read the scripture, study the context, if necessary get help in understanding it. Don't just accept it because it sounds right.

Satan takes Jesus up on a high pinnacle of the temple, and says, "If you are the Son Of God, throw yourself down from here." Satan coyly, adds, quoting Psalm 91:11, "For it is written:" mockingly copying Jesus' own words, "He shall give His angels charge over

125

you, to keep you." Then from Psalm 91:12, "In their hands they shall bear you up, lest you dash your foot against a stone."

Jesus doesn't let Satan get away with using the scripture incorrectly. Jesus came back with an answer from God's Word that would put Satan's quote in the proper context and in balance with the whole Word of God. Quoting, Deuteronomy 6:16, "You shall not test the Lord your God."

There are all kinds of devils out there that quote scripture. Many times they want to take an obscure verse and take it out of context to create a new teaching or revelation. We must understand the whole counsel of God. The teaching should be consistent with God's teaching and His nature.

Not that long ago, a young man appeared and said he was Christ returned. He said that the world had refused to accept the sinless Son of God, so now he had come as the "sinful" savior. The red flags should have been waving to anyone familiar with God's divine nature and character. Those who follow this

Christ paid dearly with their lives and the lives of their loved ones. We must be students of the Word.

Jesus knew and used the Word of God to defeat every thrust of Satan's temptations. We, too, must use the Word for our defense and as a weapon.

TAKING A CLOSE LOOK AT OUR WEAPON

In a sword fight, the sword is both a weapon and a defense. The sword is used both to destroy the enemy and to fend off the swordplay of the enemy. The enemy will thrust and the defender must deflect or parry the thrust before striking their own blow. In the temptation of Jesus we see the Word used both defensively and as a weapon to drive off the enemy.

Our sword is used the same way. Jesus used the Word both defensively and offensively. Jesus used the Word to protect Himself from acting presumptuously. The Word gives a plan and direction for our lives. The Bible tells us how to live. That is why it is important to read and to study it.

In Luke 4:4, Jesus answers Satan's temptation to turn the stones to bread, by saying, "It is written that man shall not live by bread alone.." How should we live? "By every word of God." Our lives should follow the teaching of the Word of God.

Jesus is saying to the devil, I will not allow you or anyone else, other than God, to dictate how I should act. I will not act on my own will. I will live my life according to the words and the direction of Almighty God.

In life, as Christians we are trying to follow God's plan for our life. We are living according to the teachings of His Word. When the devil comes to attack and begins to try to undermine our faith by telling us we are in the wrong place or have done the wrong thing, we can stand up and parry that attack with the fact, that we, too, live according to God's word.

The Word, too, is used offensively in this same context. It determines our conduct in life. When the enemy comes tempting us to do wrong, we can defeat the impact of that temptation by holding on to the fact that we will not follow the desires of our flesh or the influences of the world but that we will follow the teachings and precepts of God's Word.

The Holy Spirit's Help In Using The Sword

In Matthew 10:19, Jesus tells us not to worry when we have to answer those who challenge us. He said that we would be given the words to speak. How does that happen? When Jesus was speaking of the coming comforter, the Holy Spirit, in John 14:26, He said, that the Holy Spirit would bring to our remembrance all the things that He (Jesus) had said.

Jesus described the Holy Spirit as a helper. The Spirit helps us as we read the Word of God. He helps both to understand and to remember. We should ask the Lord to help us as we study His Word. To put that Word not just into our heads but also into our hearts, so that when the enemy comes and he begins one of his scurrilous attacks, we find the right scripture being brought to our remembrance by the Holy Spirit.

The Holy Spirit makes our weapons mighty. It is the Spirit that empowers to fight and makes our words, words of life and death. The Holy Spirit can make words come alive to the hearer. Those words become like barbs that penetrate into the soul of the unbeliever. Words that the hearer cannot get away from, can't escape. The Words of God spoken by the believer, anointed by the Spirit are potent weapons to defeat the hold of the enemy.

The Spirit can make our words into two-edged swords to pierce the unbelieving heart. Words that bring about conviction, then enlightenment and birth desire for change. The Word of God fitly spoken is truly a mighty weapon.

THE PRACTICAL APPLICATION

<u>Stay</u> Full Of The Holy Spirit..

We need to be people who stay full of the Holy Spirit. We need to follow Paul's command to worship. Worship is not just a Sabbath activity. We should wake up every morning and begin to praise the Lord. We need to have praise tapes in our homes and in our cars. Play the tape and join in. Let the

Holy Spirit fill you to overflowing and He will use you to touch others.

<u>Study</u> The Word..

We must become people of the Word. We need to study and understand the scriptures. We need the help of God to bring forth changes in ourselves and in our willingness to share the Word with others.

We need to read the Bible. We should have a set plan and time to incorporate the Word into our lives. If we read and study just three chapters a day, we can read the entire bible through in one year.

We need to study the Word. We have marvelous tools at our disposal to help us understand the Word. Every believer should have the basic books to help him understand the Word. A bible dictionary, a complete concordance and a one-volume commentary are the minimum helps.

Before you start to read or study, take time to **pray**. Ask the Lord to use the Holy Spirit to make the

Word come alive to you. Ask Him to speak directly to you from some passage that you will read that day. Ask the help of the Spirit to put those words to work in your life and to keep them in remembrance in your spirit.

<u>Show</u> The Word By Living It..

We need to be people who live the Word of God. When we study the Word and see areas of our lives don't match up to the Scripture, we must change. Ask the Lord to help you incorporate that teaching into your life. We need to make a commitment to God that we will be obedient to His Word and then do it.

<u>Share</u> The Word..

Use the Bible to begin to open the eyes of unbelievers. We meet people everyday that are hurting. We need to be ready to speak words of encouragement and comfort to hurting and lost people. From our few words, there may be birthed an opportunity to share the gospel of salvation. If not, we have planted a living seed that could bring forth a harvest at a later time.

We should do our best to be ready to share the gospel. If it is hard to share our faith, carry tracts or invite people to come to church. Take the battle to the enemy's territory in some way.

CHAPTER NINE

BEING STRONG IN THE LORD

EPHESIANS 6:10-20

There is an old football story about the coach who calls in his assistant during the recruiting season. The coach tells him he needs to go out and find the best athletes. The assistant asks what kind of player he should recruit to meet the team needs. The coach wants to motivate the assistant.

The coach says, "You know the kind of player that gets knocked down and gets back up?" The assistant says, "Sure. Is that kind of player we want, Coach?"

The coach answers, "No. Do you know the kind of player that gets knocked down, he gets back up, and he gets knocked down again, he gets back up again?" The assistant says, "Yes. Is that the kind of player we want, Coach?

The coach says, "No. Do you know the kind of player that gets knocked down, he gets back up, he gets knocked down again, he gets back up again, and he gets knocked down a third time and he still gets back up?" The assistant says, "Yes sir, is that the kind of player we want, coach.?"

The coach says, "No, we don't want him either. I want you to find the guy who's knocking everybody down. That's the guy we want."

The world has the wrong idea about Christianity. The world tends to think of Christians being weak. It is the idea of a bunch of old fuddy-duddies with little pot bellies and bifocals sitting around with nothing better to do than go to church and sing a few songs and hear someone read from the Bible. Unfortunately, for some Christians, their perspective isn't much better. Sadly, many Christians really don't understand what they have been called to do.

Listen, this is what the Bible teaches about the Church and Christians. The Bible says, that the Lord Jesus Christ is building a great Church, a Church that is going to do battle with the powers of Hell. This Church is made up of men and women intent on winning the spiritual battle. Christians are to be part of God's Army. Christians are called to determine the course of this world. To be a part of this powerful army of God requires a great deal of discipline and strength.

In Ephesians chapter six, it is clear, the Lord is speaking to His people, through the pen of Paul. The Lord tells us to take a stand, to be armored up, to take our shield and sword and be ready. We are in a life and death struggle for the souls of men and women. If we are going to fight the devil and his forces, if we expect to stand against the spiritual powers of darkness, if we are going to win the war, we must be **Strong.**

The key to this chapter and the key for Christians in the spiritual battle is found in verse ten. The words here almost become a shout of instruction, the army being drilled and prepared for the battle. Our Commander speaks, "Be Strong."

BE STRONG

Why be strong? We are told why. Look at verse eleven; be strong that you might stand against the wiles of the enemy. There were Indian nations in the Americas that judged the strength of various tribes by the strength of their enemies. We must be strong because we fight against powerful forces.

Who is our enemy? It is Satan. Satan is a real being. We live in a day where everything is doubted. Don't doubt this. Satan is a real spiritual being and he is out to destroy you and everyone you love. If you believe the Bible, if you believe Jesus Christ, then you must believe that there is a terrible, malignant force at work in this world, empowered and led by Satan. Now what are we to do about it?

When Satan attacks us we must stand up and fight back. Satan will attack. He will come against us in various ways. The devil has his wiles or schemes. What are they? Satan uses fear, doubt, and misery. Satan wants to destroy the witness of believers in the world. He wants to make them ineffective, so that they will not have any effect on the rest of mankind and so that they might even become so disillusioned that they fall back into his clutches.

Satan's Key Weapon Is Deception

Satan's primary weapon against believers is deception. Satan is a liar. Jesus says, in John 8:44, that Satan is the father of all liars. There is the old joke about shyster-lawyers. How can you tell if a "shyster" is lying? The answer is if his lips move. How do we know if Satan is trying to deceive us? If he speaks to you, then he is trying to deceive you. When he comes whispering in our ears, count on it, it is a lie.

Satan will come whispering. He says we are unworthy. Why? Because we are worthy. We have been made worthy by the blood of Christ. He wants us to believe that we are unworthy, so that we won't draw close to God. So that we won't take our place in the battle lines. So we won't do anything. He says we have no faith. Why? Because the truth is, we do have faith. He doesn't want us to act on our faith and lay hold of the power of God. Satan is a liar. Don't listen to him and certainly, do not allow the devil's words to influence your feelings or actions. We must remember we are under attack.

In verse twelve, Paul describes our enemy and the spiritual battlefield. Paul describes a spiritual hierarchy that is at work against the plan of God and against God's people. Paul is saying we are at war. **Christians** are on the frontlines. He goes on to say we must take a stand, put on our whole armor and fight back.

As Christians, we must learn this great truth. When we come under attack, we must learn to stand our ground. We will be attacked. We can't allow the devil's attack to turn us aside. Too often, we allow the attack to make us introspective. The attack causes us to withdraw and spend valuable time reevaluating our spiritual condition. We begin to examine ourselves. What did we do wrong? Have we displeased God? Did we fail to pray enough? That gives the enemy the advantage. We must stand.

We can stand because we have put on the whole armor of God. We know the truth. We have put on the breastplate of righteousness. We are righteous through the work of Christ on the cross. We don't have to question our worthiness. We are attacked because of whom we serve not because of who we are or the way we act. We know the truth. We know that Jesus Christ is our Lord and Savior, God come in the flesh, the Son of Our Father in Heaven, the Creator of the heavens and the earth, Who has come to destroy the works of the devil. We know the truth. The Truth, that the same Jesus has called us, His Church, to go forth and continue His ministry. We expect attack but we stand and fight.

WE MUST BE STRONG AND WE MUST PRAY

We must be strong, but, there is more. In verses eighteen to twenty, Paul says, we must PRAY. It is never enough to put on the armor and stand. We must also fight. How do we fight? Well, this battle is not carnal. It is not flesh and blood we fight against but spiritual powers. So, we must fight in the spiritual realm. We fight through our prayers. The armor is directly linked to prayer.

The Lord, through Paul, is stressing that there is more to life than just what we see. There are other forces at work. We must protect ourselves and those that we love and we must fight back. Paul says, "Praying always with all prayer and supplication in the Spirit." Paul here is placing special emphasis on supplication in the Spirit. Paul is saying, in spiritual warfare there are two kinds of prayer. There is supplication in the Spirit and all other kinds of prayer.

What Is Supplication?

Supplication is making specific requests to God. Asking God to do His will on earth is not a specific prayer. Asking God to use us in bringing forth conviction and salvation in our best friend's life is specific. Things are not going to change unless we pray. It is only through prayer that we can defeat the enemy.

If the Lord's prayer is our model and we truly want to see God's will done on earth as it is done in heaven, then we need to know what the Lord wants done at this precise moment. We need to be led of the Holy Spirit in our prayers. Sometimes we pray amiss. We ask God to do things that later on we realize were not the best thing for us or the kingdom.

We need to know when the enemy is at work in a situation or whether it is just the selfish acts of man. We need our spiritual eyes and ears opened to the spiritual realm. If we don't see that some spiritual imp is at work bringing discord in a relationship, we might just blame it on immaturity or some other human frailty and pray incorrectly. We might ask God to give us patience and help the other person to grow, when we need to be asking God to set them free from spiritual oppression.

We can see that this is a need by Paul's prayers for the Church in Colossae. In Colossians (1:9), Paul prays that the believers would have knowledge of God's will in all wisdom and spiritual understanding. We can't pray God's specific will, if we don't know His will. We can't know how to pray in specific situations if we don't have the wisdom to understand what is truly happening. We need spiritual understanding.

Let's make it plain. There are a whole lot of people, including a tremendous number of Christians, who don't even believe that there is a devil or demons. If they believe in the spiritual realm, they think that the devil is at work in Asia or South America but not in "Christian" United States. Probably half of those who know and believe in spiritual warfare don't know how to fight. There are Christians who act as if they are afraid to mention Satan's name.

We need our eyes opened. There is a spiritual realm. This world and its inhabitants are being affected by the things that take place in that realm. Christians have been called to fight the forces of the evil one. We must be aware of the devil's tactics and actions. We must learn to recognize his methods and his attacks. We need to tune in to the spiritual world that is all around us.

Notice That It Is Supplication.. In The Spirit

The simplest definition of prayer is conversation with God. Conversation involves both speaking and hearing. We need to **hear** from God. We need in our prayer times to take time to just sit quietly and wait on the Lord. God will speak to you. We need to take a note pad with us to our pray times. We should be prepared to pray about specific situations. We should have jotted down the areas of concerns that are affecting us, our family, our church and the world. At the same time, we have paper and pen to make note of things that God reveals to us.

In prayer, most of us have experienced where things we hadn't planned on praying about, are brought to our conscious thinking. That is not a good memory at work. That is the Holy Spirit revealing the Lord's will in your prayers. In Romans (8:26-27), we are told that the Spirit helps us to pray.

There are times we don't know what to pray. We aren't sure how to deal with a specific problem. We know that God does know how to deal with the problem. The Spirit is there to help us pray.

In I Corinthians 14:14-15, Paul writes of praying in tongues, he says, "For if I pray in a tongue, my spirit prays, but my understanding is unfruitful. What is the conclusion then? I will pray with the Spirit, and I will also pray with understanding." Paul was saying, there are times we pray and we don't even understand what we are praying. Maybe we don't need to know but we still need to pray.

In Ephesians chapter six, verse nineteen, Paul gives us an example of specific prayer. Paul asks for prayer for himself. Paul writes, "Pray for me. Pray that utterance may be given to me, that I will speak boldly, and make known the gospel." He goes on to say a couple of other things, but he is closing his letter with an emphasis on praying specifically for him.

Why pray for Paul? Paul knew God's will for his life. He knew his mission. He had been called to make known the gospel to the Gentiles. He kept his calling close to his heart. It always took preference. He saw that mission as encompassing the care of the churches. He knew that the Church needed leadership to model Christ both to the world and to the individual believer. He knew the critical importance of leadership.

In spiritual warfare we need to pray for leadership. The leaders of our churches need to be visionaries. They need to have a clear understanding of the will of God for themselves and for their church. Leadership needs to see beyond the immediate to catch a vision of both God and His plan for the future. We must pray for the Leadership.

We must pray that they will be **Bold.** We need church leaders to step out in faith and do great things for God. We need church leaders to bring their people into the knowledge of this war. We can't afford to be timid in the things of God. We need to pray that the leaders of our churches attempt things that cannot be done unless God is in it.

Were the prayers of Paul answered? Yes, Paul did speak boldly. Through Paul's ministry to the churches, the frontiers of the gospel were pushed through the known world. It was through Paul's personal ministry and his letters that the gospel invaded both Asia and Europe. Paul not only helped change the world then, he is still doing it today. His letters, anointed by the Holy Spirit, instruct us even today on how to live and fight the good fight.

Let's Get Practical.. We Must Be Strong And Pray

We are in a war. This is a fight to the finish. Souls are at stake. We must **Be Strong**. We must **Stand** and not be turned aside. The Lord has given us all we need to stand, fight and win. If we stand our ground, the Lord will strengthen us and give us victory. Remember, Be Strong and Stand.

We are going to get attacked. Sometimes the enemy may even knock us for a loop. That can happen. When it does, get back up. Make a stand. You say, "You knocked me down. So what? I am now up. I serve a great God. He loves me and will give me victory. I will win."

The great bare-knuckles champion, Jim Jeffries was not the biggest nor the best fighter. When asked how he did it, he said, the key to winning is to keep getting up. Everybody gets knocked down. The key is to get back up. The winner is always the last man standing.

Remember, too, that we are not just to stand our ground but we are to **Fight**. We fight through Prayer. We need to keep our eyes open and we are aware of the attack of the enemy. We fight back through our prayer. We get God and the resource of heaven involved in the situation.

We know God's will for our lives and for the immediate moment. When we pray and we listen to God we begin to understand how we should pray. Then we pray accordingly. We pray specifically for our God's will to be done on earth as it is in heaven. We pray for our church, leadership, and for God's work in this world.

We are strong through Christ. We are fighting to win. The victory shall be ours.

CHAPTER TEN

WINNING THE BATTLE OF LIFE

EPHESIANS 6:18

In Ephesians chapter six, verse eighteen, Paul writes, "Praying always with all prayer and supplication in the Spirit, being watchful to this end with all perseverance and supplication for all the saints.."

Paul has been writing to the church. The Holy Spirit has led him to instruct the church both in how to please God and be a body of believers who could impact the world. He warns the church that they are in a battle. He instructs believers in how to be prepared for spiritual conflict. Make a stand, put on the God-given armor, take up the shield and sword and **Pray**.

The church is in a war and it must pray. Not just pray but make supplication, pray specifically for needs, not just for yourself but for all the saints, that is the whole body of Christ. Pray specifically. This is written in the context of spiritual warfare. What then should we pray?

WARFARE PRAYER

There are some basic principles that are evident as we begin to speak of warfare prayer. If we are going to pray against the spiritual powers that are at work against the Church and Christians we are assuming certain things both about ourselves and about this world. These assumptions are important both to our faith and to our ability to accomplish the things we are trying to do through our prayers.

First, We Believe There Is A Devil And We Oppose Him..

First, we are acknowledging that we truly believe that there is a spiritual realm. We need to recognize that a spiritual realm coexists with our physical and natural world. We are acknowledging that we believe that the world is not what it seems. We are looking beyond the ordinary and addressing the reality of unseen forces that are at work in our lives. Forces that many times are opposed to us on every level and that may be exerting their will against us in many different ways.

Why is that significant? Satan prefers to work behind a veil of secrecy. He prefers the world not only to be blind to God and the hope of salvation, Second Corinthian 4:4, but he prefers that the world is oblivious to him and his minions. Satan does not want the unbeliever to know that he is real. If Satan exists, if he is real, it begs the question as to the reality of God.

More to the point, if the believer is aware and actually looking for satanic opposition, then there is less chance for the devil to defeat them. Unfortunately, the spiritual forces of the devil are mostly unopposed in their influence and attacks on the church and the believer. No wonder Paul says, "*Be* watchful to this end with all perseverance.."

We need to keep our spiritual eyes open for the influences of the evil one. We need to be on guard for his attack that we might "pray" against him and his schemes and see victory through Christ.

Secondly, We Believe That Our God Reigns Over All Creation..

In coming to the place of recognizing the hand of the devil in his attacks against the Church and individual believers and then praying for God's help and direction in countering that attack, we are also acknowledging that we believe that our God has the power and authority over all forces of the enemy.

This is very important. Remember, Satan and his followers use deception and fear as their primary weapons. The forces of the evil one want you to believe that you are powerless against them and their attack. They want to instill fear into you so that you will not oppose them.

Our willingness to pray and ask our Lord to intercede on our behalf or to empower us to fight against these evil spirits disarms them. It takes away their strength and primary modes of attack. We have pre-disposed them to defeat before we start.

We are standing on the promises of the Word of God, where we are told that Jesus "disarmed" the spiritual powers at the cross and that we are no longer in bondage. We now stand empowered to defeat the attack of the enemy.

We can stand and declare, "You evil spirit, you have been defeated at the cross. You have to bow your knees before Christ, the exalted Son of God, and acknowledge that you have no authority over me as a believer or over those I claim in the Name Of Christ Jesus my King."

Thirdly, We Believe That Our Prayers Can Make A Difference..

When we go to prayer against the forces of darkness, we are, also, acknowledging that we believe that our prayers will make a difference. We are praying because we believe that our God will move heaven and earth in our behalf to defeat the powers that oppose the work and ministry of the church.

Again, this is significant, because Satan and his imps want to destroy your faith. They don't want you to pray. They are constantly trying to undermine our faith by telling us we have no faith or that God won't answer because we are unworthy. The devil will do anything to stop you from praying and believing that God will answer your prayers. Why? Because if you don't pray or if you don't believe that God cares, then you will be defeated before you start.

The very fact that you are praying indicates that you have faith in God and believe that He will answer your prayers. If not then why pray. We are acknowledging our "faith" by being people of prayer. We are saying to God and to all creation, "Yes, I believe that my prayers make a difference because my Lord both hears and answers my petitions. "

Our Prayers can change this situation. Our prayers can change this community, this city, this state, this nation, this world. We pray because we believe that we can defeat the enemy and make a real difference.

THE PATTERN OF SPIRITUAL WARFARE PRAYER

We, as Christians, have come to a place in our lives where we have made Jesus Christ, our Lord and Savior. We don't do anything of ourselves. We fully expect the Lord, through the ministry of the Holy Spirit to lead us. Proverbs 16:9 tells us, that the Lord directs our steps. We want and need the help of the Holy Spirit in our daily lives and in the decisions that we must make in this world. Similarly, we want the Spirit to guide us in our confrontations with the demonic forces.

We need to seek the Spirit's leading in our prayers. Paul specifically mentions in Ephesians 6:18, we are to pray with all prayers and supplications in the Spirit. The Lord will help us. We will find the words flowing from our spirit and mind as the Holy Spirit brings them to our consciousness.

Again, there are steps we should take in entering into the battle prayer. A biblical approach both builds our faith and gives us confidence in the spiritual battle, a simple pattern for our spiritual warfare prayer. The pattern we have chosen is quite easy to remember. It is as easy as "A" "B" "C" "D". If we just remember those letters and what they refer to, we can approach the battle with confidence.

A. <u>Affirm</u> Your Faith In Christ

In spiritual warfare, we need to affirm our complete reliance and faith in Jesus Christ. We don't go into battle in our own strengths. We go forth as representatives of our Lord. We bear His name. We are Christians serving the King of Kings.

In Ephesians chapter one, Paul writes of our position in Christ. Paul begins in verse three saying we are blessed. He goes on to say that God chose us before He ever created the universe and that God dearly loves us. In verse five, Paul states that we are children of God. In verses six and seven, he declares that we are accepted in "Christ" and forgiven. In verse nine, we are told that God has a purpose for us that He has made known through the revelation of His will.

Paul has laid the foundation for the church. He wants us to see our position in the kingdom established not by any effort of our own but by the work of Jesus Christ. The Lord has a divine purpose for each of our lives. A plan that the Lord is revealing to us that we might fulfill His will. He establishes these truths and then goes on to explain our role in expanding the Kingdom of God and fighting the spiritual war.

It all begins with our position in Christ. We have given Jesus Christ full authority over our lives. Christ has accepted us and He has with that authority also taken responsibility for us. He will not allow us to face anything that we can't handle, I Corinthians 10:13, and He will see us through to our ultimate victory. We have no cause for fear. We are where the Lord wants us and He is with us to see that we fulfill His plan.

B. <u>Believe</u> You Are Empowered By The Holy Spirit..

Later in Ephesians chapter one, in verses eighteen to twenty-three, Paul points to the fact that the church and the individual Christian has received an anointing of power from God. In verse sixteen, Paul says he has been praying for the church. He has been asking God to open their eyes to the benefits that they have through Christ Jesus. In verse nineteen, Paul writes of the great power that is working in us who believe, the same measure as the power that raised Christ from the dead.

This is very important; the Lord is using Paul to instruct the church, He is describing the Power of God that is available to us. In verse twenty-one, the power that is available to each and every believer is compared to the power of Satan's kingdom. That verse states, "far above ALL principality and power and might and dominion, and every name that is named, not only in this age but also in that which is to come."

We have the Holy Spirit, the power of God, working toward, in and through us. In those verses, Paul uses every power word he can think of until he runs out of words. He is looking for the right analogy. He goes back to the ultimate confrontation between

God and Satan. He goes back to the cross and the tomb. We can almost hear Paul, "This power that works in the believer it is like.. the power that raised Christ from the dead." That same power tore apart the spiritual kingdom of darkness and made an open shame of all the enemies of God. We have that power.

Sometimes, Christians act like they are afraid of the devil. They quote Jude 9, where it says that Michael the archangel dared not bring an accusation against the devil. They reason that if an archangel was afraid, then we should be afraid, too. We don't have the spirit of an archangel to help us, we have the Holy Spirit, God, to stand against and work through us in our battles against Satan's forces. Let the devils and imps fear the Spirit-filled believer. Remember, you have been empowered by God.

When you walk onto the battlefield, you do not walk in defenseless; you walk on in the full regalia and armor of the Lord of lords and the King of kings. You stand ready, empowered by the Holy Spirit, to fight and to win.

C. Remember The <u>Cross</u>.. Through It Satan Was Defeated..

We are not only empowered, our Lord and Savior, Jesus Christ has already defeated the enemy for us. Remember Colossians 2:15, speaking of Christ's work at the cross, "Having disarmed principalities and powers, He (Jesus) made a public spectacle of them, triumphing over them in it. Jesus has disarmed the spiritual powers that work against us. He has taken their power and authority over us away from them. He has made an open spectacle of them.

That Satan has been made an open spectacle is worthy of closer examination. It is like the children's story about the emperor who wore no clothes. Satan had convinced the entire world to fear him. Jesus came and through the cross showed the devil's true nature and character. All creation saw him stripped of his disguises and deceptions, Satan became an open spectacle.

There is more, in Hebrews 2:14-15, it says, speaking of Jesus and His work at the cross, "..He Himself likewise shared in the same (death), that through death

He might destroy him who had the power of death, the devil, and releases those who through fear of death were all their lifetime subject to bondage." Jesus broke the hold, the power that Satan had over us through His own death. Jesus has left Satan powerless to defeat us, who believe on Jesus, and walk in His divine plan.

Remember the old horror movies, where the hero would hold up the cross against the dreaded bloodsucker. Well, we too, hang on to the cross. We hold it up to remind both us and the enemy that the battle has been won and that we enjoy the fruits of victory.

D. We <u>Defeat</u> Spiritual Powers Through Prayer..

We never enter the battle alone. The Lord has promised to be with us all of our lives and until the end of the age. We have a God who wants to be and is involved in our everyday lives. Still, we are creatures of a free will. We can choose to fight our battles alone or we can call on the Lord and bring God and all the resource of heaven to bear on the situation. To win the battle, we need to allow the Lord to help us.

God has given us authority over the enemy and access to the throne of God. In Luke 10:19, speaking to His disciples, the Lord said, "Behold, I give you the authority to trample over serpents and scorpions, and over all power of the enemy, and nothing shall by any means hurt you." We have the power and the authority to face the enemy and to win. So what must we do?

1. Bind The Enemy. In Luke 11, we see Jesus casting out a demon. Some said that Jesus cast out the demon by demonic power. Jesus answered the charges by saying that a house divided soon falls. He went on to say that if one was going to take what a strong man had, that he had better first "bind" the strong man. This is obviously in the context of coming against spiritual powers.

In Matthew 18:18, speaking of spiritual discipline, it says what the believer binds on earth is bound in heaven. We can deter, hold back, bind the enemy we fight in the spirit, by binding him through the authority given us by Jesus. In prayer and by faith bind the strong forces of Satan that hinder us in completing God's plan.

2. Pull Down Strongholds. In Second Corinthians 10:4-5, we are told our weapons are not carnal, fleshly but spiritual for the pulling down of strongholds. There are strongholds within and without.

We have allowed the world and the enemy to build strongholds in our minds. These wrong ideas have come through inaccurate and wrong teaching we have received from various sources. We have been influenced by well-meaning public educators and by everything we have read or seen. These ideas are ingrained in our thinking and many times oppose the truth of the gospel. Sometimes, sin has entrenched itself in our thinking and we have rationalized ourselves into thinking it is okay. We need to pull down any stronghold of wrong thinking.

We need also to come against spiritual powers ingrained in the fabric of our community. These strongholds exist where Satan has control over non-believers. Satan and his followers may be influencing your local city government, your state politics. The enemy may have a network of spiritually deceived followers fighting against your every move both in the natural realm and in the supernatural world. We need the help of God to break and pull down these strongholds.

3. Break Every Evil Or Demonic Curse. Galatians 3:10-13, states, that we were once under the curse of the law. There are curses that affect our lives. There are curses that come through sin and wrong activity. In Galatians 6:7, says, that what a man sows he shall also reap. The curses of our former lives were broken at the cross. Some curses are spoken against us when we are children. These words are buried in our subconscious mind but they work against us. Some curses are spoken against us or God's work by those aligned with Satan. We need to ask God to break any curse and to make it of no effect both in the minds of those who heard it and in its purpose against us.

4. Send The Evil Spirits That Fight Against Us Into The Abyss. We know that evil spirits fight against us. We need to vanquish these spirits. Is that possible? In Luke 8:31, Jesus meets a man who had a "legion" of spirits possessing him. Jesus starts to cast them out and the spirits beg not to be sent to the pit. Jesus said we would do His works. So why can't we send those spirits that come against us into the pit? If they dreaded this possibility, then we should do our best to see it come to pass and then they won't bother us again.

5. Ask God To Send His Angels To Encamp Around Us And Those That We Love. Psalm 34:7, states, "The angel of the Lord encamps around those who fear Him and delivers them." We must feel more confident in our spiritual battles if the angels of the Lord watch over us. We need all the help we can get to accomplish the plan of God. We need protection and at times, we need deliverance.

There is a wonderful story of a young woman working in the mean streets of New York. One night, coming home late from the ministry, two unsavory characters follow her. As she entered her darkened street, the two men ordered her to stop and demanded her purse. Suddenly the two muggers turned and ran. Later, one of the two told the police of a strange man chasing them away with a sword. The young woman had seen no one else in the street but believed that an angel had come to her rescue.

We can ask the Lord to send His angels to help us in the battle and to stand guard over us. We can then stand on the promise of deliverance found in Psalm 34:7.

6. Ask It All In The Name Of Our Lord Jesus Christ. When we pray we need to affirm our relationship with God through His Son, Jesus Christ. We need to do this NOT to remind the Lord but to build our own faith and confidence. We are a people intent on fulfilling the teachings of our Lord. We want to know His will and do it. We want to grow and become mature, strong believers who take their place in the church and on the battle lines. We fully trust that we are children of God and that He will bring forth His victory through us.

We, also, remind the enemy of who we are in Christ. Every foul spirit must hate to hear that precious name. Our old natures are replicas of the nature of Satan. We are selfish, he is selfish. We are "sore losers" and he and his followers are sore losers. They don't want to be reminded of their conqueror. They hate to hear Him praised. So we need to lift up His name at every opportunity. We need to sing His praises and declare that Jesus is our Lord.

The Practical Application

Prayer is the absolute vital key to victory in the spiritual realm. We are at WAR. We must pray. It is through prayer that we bring forth the power and the resource of God.

Remember the simple "**ABC**"s

A to Affirm our faith in Christ.

B to Believe that we are empowered by the Holy Spirit.

C to look to the Cross where our victory was established.

D to Defeat the spiritual powers through prayer.

SATAN'S ULTIMATE END

We shall win the battles and ultimately the war. One day our Lord Jesus will return and eliminate sin and the great sinner, Satan. In Revelations 20:1-3, we are told of the end of the last great battle. Jesus has defeated the armies of man and the armies of Satan by simply speaking words of destruction. Jesus then sends an angel to lay hold of Satan and bind him. Satan will be dragged back before the King of Kings and the Lord of Lords, to be sentenced. The enemy that once created so much dread and pain brought in chains to the feet of our Lord. Satan is already defeated. He knows that and we should too. We win the war. God is calling us to win the battles.

THE END

CPSIA information can be obtained
at www.ICGtesting.com
Printed in the USA
LVHW081043170922
728615LV00031B/1003